Yeah, Baby.

By J. Wolfendale

This book is in loving memory of Mad Dave,

my dear friend.

ISBN: 978-1-84753-204-6

Vive le Punk

'Monday i've got Friday on my mind'. Good song. I was living in a guest house in Leighton Buzzard. It was 1981. Getting dressed in my cramped little room in the eaves. Listening to Soft Cell singing 'Bedsitter' on my record player. It sat on my armchair. There was no room for a table. I had all my records on the floor. Everything from Elvis to the Pistols. 25 years of Rock and Roll. On with my Anarchy shirt and trousers. New black Pixie boots. We'd pinched them from outside a shop in Luton the week before. On with the black eyeliner and nail varnish. A bit of lipstick to finish. I always wore a safety pin through my ear. Silver to match my studded belt. My friend Tony came up from his room downstairs.To see if i wanted to eat with him before we went out. I went down to eat. The Ramones album 'It's Alive' was playing.

He always seemed to look after me. Tony. He was boxing champion. Drummer in the band. Leader of the Punks. The chairman. My friend. Since we met at boxing club. When we were little. Last week a couple of older blokes dragged me down the alley as I came out of the Pub at closing time. I had a good go but i was no match for them. They didn't like punks and were giving me a good kicking. Tony hurried up. He knocked them both over without a word. One punch each. Bang bang. The Stooges 'Search and Destroy' was drifting out of the side window. Honestly. It's one of those things you remember.

I had some vegetarian food he'd cooked. Unusual in those days. Off we went. Down the pub. Through the door and we were in. There they all were. The Leighton Punx, the Bedford Punks, and The Luton Punks. Studs, zips, safety pins, chains, torn shirts, multi coloured hair. Punk was not yet the uniform of ripped jeans, leather jacket and mohican haircuts. You weren't supposed to all look the same. I had jet black hair. I wore make up. I wore a kilt and fishnets with studded biker boots. Parachute shirt. Designer clothes. Sometimes i was told i looked more like a New Romantic. Marc Almond from Soft Cell. They had just come out as the new thing. I didn't care. I thought they were great. They did a cover of a Northern Soul song. It was all dressing up to me. I bumped into Steve Strange in the Vivienne Westwood shop last week. Down the Kings Road. In Chelsea. He's got a band. Visage. I think they're great. I sort of know him from gigs and stuff. He told me when they're playing at the Blitz club. Have to go down to that.

The Clash were singing 'Clash City Rockers' on the jukebox. In the corner sat the Leighton Skinheads. It was The Leighton Carnival. We were playing at the Bossard Hall . Backing up The Subhumans. They walked in about ten minutes later. This was what we'd all been waiting for. It seemed like weeks. What a buzz. Being in that pub was like having our own little world. Our own Family. We all fitted in. It was happy. It was escape. We all spent the week waiting for Friday. The weekend was our life. Seemed like we went to a different gig every week. The list would be long ; The Clash, The Jam, The Banshees, The

Cure,The Ants, Stiff little Fingers, Madness and The Specials, hundreds more.
We still got paid weekly in cash . So did everyone then. That or the Dole.

The concert was excellent. Good sound , crowd going crazy. The night seemed to last forever. I flailed away at my Rickenbacker guitar. Trying to do a Pete Townsend. Great review in the fanzine the next month . It said I played a good guitar. Hmm. This was theatre. I loved it. This was what it was all about . Like the Mods 20 years earlier. Escaping the greyness of life by dressing up. Pretending to be someone else. Every day. Nothing to do with politics. Nothing to do with drawing attention . There were easier ways to get a smack in the mouth . I ended up going home with a punk girl . She had been staring at me the whole time i was playing. After the gig she followed me around. There were groupies. Even on our small scale. Very flattering .It was always nicer to wake up next to someone. Her mum made us breakfast in the morning. We lay in bed listening to Lou Reed's 'Rock and roll animal'. Now that's a good guitar.

Another weekend. Down at the Bossard Hall. It's Ian's 21st birthday. He's got UKDecay from Luton playing. They're a real popular band. LP and everything. We're all down the front. It's packed solid. The music starts. The singer Abbo's got Tartan punk clothes. Brothel creepers. Big backcombed hair. They start their song 'Middle of the road man'. That intro is great. Spon's crashing guitar. Tony's watching Their drummer, Steve Harle. He's very good. Tony's shadow boxing to the beat. As he would. They're his favourite band. They are very good. Abbo's twirling his studded belt around above his head. What a front man. The audience goes mad. Belts flying everywhere. It's the Luton Belts. Their own fan club. They follow the band around The music is putting the hairs up on the back of my neck. I swear. Ian gets up on stage. The Chorus. Abbo's got his arm round Ian's shoulders. Singing 'Do you like Ugg' That's Ian's nickname. Everyone is cheering. What a great party. Seemed to go so quickly. About midnight. I'm walking home down Doggett Street. There's two guys playing a Piano under a streetlight in the rain. Laughing. It's Jake and Nige. They are pissed out of their heads. They wheeled it out of the hall after the gig. Noone said a word. Blimey.That was fun.

The following week i went over to Bedford to meet some friends. I was sitting in the Cadena cafe in the arcade, drinking a pot of tea. I used to go up there to smoke when i was at school. Only 4 years earlier but already a lifetime away. On the next table sat a big meathead and his girlfriend. As i got up to leave he looked at me- "you staring at my bird mate?" No. " why, don't you fancy her then?" No. " What, are you saying she's ugly?" No. "You a queer then? You fuckin look like one" No. "So you do fancy her then" No i don't, leave me alone you cunt. I turned to go and he went to get up. Oh Fuck. Here we go then. Now or never. I picked up the stool i had been sitting on. I hit him with it three times as he came at me. He lay still on the floor. A little surprised. His girlfriend screamed at me to leave him alone. I was a thin effeminate looking 17 year old. He must have been 2 or 3 years older than me. He was two or three stone bigger. What was i supposed to do, let him hit me first and do me the damage? I always hated bullies. I walked quickly back to the train station with my legs shaking. I expected a gang of blokes to follow me any moment. I wouldn't be going back to Bedford again in a hurry then.

The next time was the infamous riot at the Bunyan centre. The Angelic Upstarts were playing. Backed up by UK Decay. They have just started. Doing their song 'Sexual'. It is blinding. All of a sudden. There's a big skinhead. Gets up on stage. Topless. StaPrest and braces. He is covered in blood. He's screaming. Seig Heil. The skins think it was the punks . It wasn't . It was the bouncers. Too late. Fuck. We are so outnumbered. Me and Tony standing back to back in the hall. Punching every bone head that came our way. I'm slapping them with my belt. Solid studs. Not like the fashion accessory pyramid stud ones. No weight to them. The fuckers won't stay down..The hall is full of people fighting. Fists. Belts. Boots. They've pulled Abbo off the stage. Steve Spon is hitting skins with his guitar on stage. Auntie Sue is swinging the mike stand. Knocking them over like skittles. Fuckin 'ell. Over by a fire exit. Captain Bluett is getting a hiding. Three skins. Me and Tony run out. They run off. Outside it's worse. Everyone 's fighting the coppers. One grabs Tony. From behind. I fire a left hook behind his ear. He goes down. That's six years of kung - fu for you. I'd been boxing with Tony a few times but it wasn't really my thing. Sometimes I ran through the woods. To meet up with Tony for a run round Stockgrove park. Road work he called it. I called it running. Whatever. The copper never saw me coming. His mate did though. He's coming at me with his truncheon. Bollocks. All of a sudden there's the big skinhead from the stage. He grabs hold of the copper and picks him up. He throws him against the wall. He's trying to stop the skins from fighting the punks. Fuck it. It's too late. Police vans and cars are getting turned over. It's the wild west. We run back to our van. Loads of Leighton punks piling in. We can hear the dogs barking now. I see the skin being dragged off. There's five coppers to do it though. He's still trying to fight them. Poor fucker. He'll be receiving some special attention in the cells then. We drive out. Very Carefully. We are waved out by a copper. Tony gives him two fingers. Home James. John Peel's playing The Only Ones on the radio. 'Another Girl Another Planet'. Spizz Energi. Where's Captain Kirk'. Excellent. The riot was on Anglia news the next night. It blamed the punks and skins. It was the bouncers though. Never believe the media.

Next day. Hungry and thirsty. I went into the cafe . Punky Suzy was working in there waitressing. She was beautiful. Like Diana Rigg in her younger days. She had black & purple hair. She had fishnets & safety pins. And her waitress coat. That was it. Nothing else underneath. As i found out when she came round later. Lost souls clinging together. We fell asleep listening to Iggy Pop. 'Turn Blue'. A night without end.

I Bought a little motorbike. Yamaha RS 100. They weren't restricted in those days. It went well. I took it up the village. To show my biker friends. It's where I grew up. They laughed. We all started out with a small one they say. Bet you've still got one i say. Wagging my little finger at them. They told me to fuck off. So i did. Laughing.
I think it was because they knew I was a Donna Summer fan that they didn't take me seriously. Why did we have to like just one sort of music ? That's like being racist or sexist. Or something. The Pistols could put the hairs up on the back of my neck with one chord. Donna Summer could make me cry with one note. Her songs were sweeping, poetic operettas about the world she moved in. Complete stories, romances, life on the street. The same way that Tom Waits sang about the dangerous, underside of America that existed like the Twilight Zone. I put them all on the turntable and escaped to other worlds with them. Like friends. Or lovers. Somewhere over the rainbow. I loved Punk. I always loved Disco. And everything in between. There are two of me. Check out Madleen Kane's 'Cherie' or Dalida's 'Gigi in Paradisco'. Boris Midney's Beautiful Bend. Masterpieces. I just knew they were having a damn good time in their night clubs. Ignoring the endless dole queues and dressing up in all those lovely sparkly clothes, partying like there was no tomorrow. We dressed down and sang about No Future. It's taken me a while to see it as that 'Glass half empty / Glass half full ' thing. Wish I'd thought of it then. I try to think positive these days. Maybe I should have been a disco queen, but I

didn't know any. I knew Punks. I guess I just wasn't happy, somewhere deep inside.........

One Friday night. Down town. After the pub. Five pints. Me and Keith. Decided to go to visit his girlfriend. In Hemel Hempstead. He didn't have a crash helmet. Fuck it. Who cares. Off we go. Just going through Dagnall. There's a cop car. This little bike. Two punks on it. All studs. Keith's pink hair blowing in the wind. It's not quick enough for a getaway. Blue light flashing. Fuck. We stop.They ask if it's mine. I show them my documents. They ask why the rear light doesn't work. They ask where Keith's crash helmet is. I'm giggling. Have you been drinking they say . Maybe a bit. Right then. Blow into this. It's one of the old breathalysers. Tube of crystals. If it turns green i'm fucked. I give it a good blow. They look at it. After five minutes it hasn't changed colour. They can't believe it. Neither can i. Well they say. Well i say. Well you can't go to Hemel with him like that. Or with no back light. Fine. I tell them I'll push it back to Leighton. We'll drive back to check they say. They don't think we're funny. They drive off. I pin the tube to my jacket lapel. With the big safety pin from my ear. We get back on. Ride on to Hemel Hempstead. Fuck 'em. No problem. Ho Ho. I wore that tube for weeks.

Punky Suzy, it went somewhere, it went wrong.....
One word .Heroin. How corny and filthy that shit is. I was falling asleep with a spliff and Pink Floyds 'the wall'. The Banshees. Steel Pulse. Whatever. We snorted crap Sulphate whenever we could find it. That was it. It was for fun. It was for escape. We all did it. I thought that Smack was

from Hip New Orleans in the 40's/50's. I thought it had died at the end of the sixties in New York. If only. How i tried to love that girl. The way only teenagers can. You know when you see someone for the first time and they take your breath away. She was that stunning. Every time i looked at her. Legs up to her ears. Everyone fancied her. It took me six months to realise she felt the same. That day in the cafe, i asked her round for a cup of tea when she finished work. She came. We fell on each other. I remember. I wish i didn't. We had such a time. She entered the local beauty contest. Fuck me she looked good. They were playing Heaven 17 – Fascist Groove Thang. The judges obviously didn't care for punks. Or her outspokenness against general apathy. I think they preferred someone who dressed like a disco dolly & wanted to help sick animals. That's who won anyway. You could see that the males in the audience had not been the ones who voted. Only with their eyes. I was proud to walk out of there with her. She outdressed me. She out classed me. She didn't out love me. Something was eating away at her. I asked the question. She lied. I knew she was lying.

We'd go out in the morning sometimes. Just as it was getting light. After being up all night speeding. Listening to The Buzzcocks. Sam and Dave . Love. I always thought that their track '7 & 7 is' was the first Punk record. Not Lou Reed. We'd wait for the milkman. Then we'd pinch milk and orange juice from peoples doorsteps. Sometimes we'd get bread too. Obvious in our bondage trousers and coloured hair. Creeping through the early morning mist. It was fun. At night we'd go to the ChineseTakeaway. At closing time. They'd give us whatever they hadn't sold. Ways to survive. One night. Outside. There's some guy. Bigger. Older. What the fuck do you look like he says. I can see his point. Kilt. Fishnets & biker boots. Destroy shirt. Black & orange hair. Make up. I hate bikers he says. I'm not a biker . Says he hates queers as well . I'm not one of those either . He says i look like a cunt anyway. Bang. I land him my best shot on the chin. He doesn't go down. Oh Fuck. He launches at me. Both fists flying. He's done this before. Fuck. There we are Dancing around. Throwing combinations at each other .Ow ! The Chinese guy from the Chippie runs out. He's got Nunchakas. His friend has got a big fish knife. Uh-Oh ! Suzy jumps on the guys back. Gouging his eyes. I've got one eye i can't see out of. And blood pouring from my nose. At last. Bang. Right on the temple. He's down. Suzy gets off. Fuck's sake he looks worse than me. The Chinese guys are laughing. Patting me on the back. I watch as the guy gets to his feet. That's some punch he says. But you still look like a cunt. Fair enough. Wanker says Suzy. Off he goes. We got loads of food that night. Ended up in the churchyard. Making love on top of an old tomb. Made me think of all those girls in the old Hammer horror films. Mmmm. Very Gothic. Or an omen.

Winter. It's been snowing for four days. There's two inches of hard packed snow on the roads. I go over to Woburn Sands to see some friends. On the way back the throttle cable snaps. Just as i get into Aspley Guise. Fuck. I'm stranded. I walk to the village phone box. Ring my friend John. Says he'll be half an hour. I sit there. Shivering and smoking. He turns up. Not in his Mum's car. On his bike. A Yamaha RD 200. Oh dear. He's got a tow rope wrapped round his waist. We look at the offending cable. It's snapped off just where it goes into the engine casing. Right then he says. I'll tow you. So we tie it around his rear grab rail and my front forks. Don't worry he says. I'll take it easy. We move off. Slowly. We take the back roads through the woods. We keep having to stop. My hand hurts. We've only got one Gauntlet each. One of his thin gloves on the other hand. It is fuckin' freezing. It gets a bit tricky going up steep hills. Sliding across the road like a pendulum. Not much grip on the snow. I've got both my feet down. Boots scraping along the snow. Finally we make it back. Can't move my right hand though. It's frozen solid. Didn't see one car. Not surprised he says. You'd have to be mad to go out in this. I suppose he had a point. Fuck my hand hurt as it warmed up. Enough to shed tears. Still. Got the bike fixed the next week.

On the way to work. Overtaking a Vauxhall Viva. Just as i get alongside it turns in front of me. Smack. Straight into the back wing. I fly over the car. Land flat on my back on the verge. I got up. Couldn't see my bike. Where the fuck had that gone. The driver comes up. Says he didn't see me. Where's my bike i say. It's slid round the corner into the entrance to Lancer Boss. I pick it up. Broken clutch lever. Broken indicator. Bent footrest. That's it. Blimey that was lucky he says. Yep i say. I get back on and ride it to work. In first gear. Insurance job. Bike gets fixed again. I got cortesone injections in my shoulder. Bikes eh ?

A month or so later. Me and John. Get invited to this party by my friend Pigsy. Don't know how he got invited. It's at a sort of approved school he says. In a Georgian country house. With a lake and everything. It's not term time. Me and John go on our bikes. Pigsy turns up in his M.G. Midget. There's loads of people there. Loads of drink. We've bought a big lump of blow with us. To start with we hide in Pigsy's car to skin up. We don't know anybody here. John could skin up with his eyes closed. After a while the smell must have drifted up to the main lawn. There's loads of people all smoking with us. We get on fine. The headmaster or someone has a key. He unlocks the mooring chain to this boat. So there we all are. Out on the lake stoned out of our heads. Drinking wine. At borstal. Ho ho. John is working like a man possessed. Just keeps passing these spliffs out. It's like a production line. Finally we are so wasted we decide to get on our bikes and go home. Pigsy says he's not fit to drive. He's not kidding. Nor are we. He's gonna sleep in his car. Can't sleep on our bikes though. No says Pigsy. Giggling. He can't even get out of his car now. Jesus. Off we go. Weaving up the long driveway. We stick very close to each other. Riding back through the country lanes. Suddenly there's a big white blur. Like a flash. Right in my face. What ! ! I'm doing 50 miles an hour. I slam on the brakes. Skid to a stop. John pulls up next to me. We pull off our crash helmets. His face looks like mine. White . Fuckin' ell he says. Did you see that ? I don't know I say. I'm wrecked. What the fuck was it. Was I seeing things ? He says he saw it. I was just dive bombed by a great white owl. Flew right into me.

Must have been my headlight. Not what you need when you're stoned. Kinda sobered me up though. Have to watch out for those killer owls man. They're everywhere. Cheech and Chong anyone ?

Another night. After a Uk Decay gig in Luton. I came back late . I walked into the flat and there's Suzy and a few friends of ours. She hadn't come. .Said she wasn't well. The Velvet Underground are singing 'Venus in Furs' There's something else too. 'What the fuck is that ?' Spoons with lighters underneath. Syringes. Fuck. I might have been naive but i sure wasn't stupid. Dog lead round her arm. Fuck. 'Get that shit out of my house'. Click. All of a sudden her new friends made sense. Her colds made sense. Her complexion, her distance made sense. She was right. She wasn't well. She lied. Again. I knew she was lying. I told the others to fuck off. They fucked off. She said she was sorry. She said she'd stop. She said she loved me more. I cried. I held her. I asked her why. She didn't stop. She couldn't tell me what was so bad in her past to need that much escape. We split up. It hurt. I was lost.

Was it someones fault? I found her dealer. I knew him. He knew me. My head went.

I kicked in his door. I broke his nose. I broke his wrist. I cracked some ribs. I trashed his flat as he watched. I told him if i came back i would kill him. I wasn't lying. I conferred with my friend John. Boot of the car. Tarpaulin. Quicksand down the woods. I told Tony. He said don't do it. He knew best. Eventually her dealer got busted. Went to prison. Maybe just as well. But she found another.

It was like a plague had come to town.The needle marks looked like vampires bites to me. It was sucking the life out of the town's young. English Gothic. At it's darkest. Seemed like everyone was on it. Me and Suzy finished for good. People were changing. Punk was dying on it's feet. New Romantics were finished. That's it then. Playtime over. No more dressing up. I cut off my dyed hair. I sold my Punk clothes. I left town. Fuck that. Suzy's Parents. They knew. They sent her to Rehab. In the country somewhere. There's a verse from Edgar Allen Poe's 'Alone' which kept going around in my head.

I reckon it about wraps it up.......

Lost

I lived with a girl. It was Ok. I tried to make her Suzy. She wasn't. Not her fault. I left and went back to Leighton. I tracked Suzy down.. I saw her. I still wanted her. It wasn't her any more. She looked the same. She looked different. There was someone else living in her body. She haunted me. The undead. I said good bye. It hurt. Again. I moved back to my parents house in the village. Too many people getting hurt. Me included.

I sold the little 100 to a friend. Bought a Suzuki GT380. Two stroke triple. That was a nice noise. I could just sit and listen to it tick over. Uneven three cylinder burble. Roared well at the red line. Me and the village bikers. Went up to London to see their friends. All screaming up the M1. We sat and smoked dope. And dried Flyagaric mushrooms. Bloody hell. That is some buzz. About two in the morning we left. Just getting the ton up past Scratchwood services. Bang. My bike starts to wobble. The back wheel locks up. I hold on for my life. They say things go in slow motion at times like that. Not for me it didn't. It skids to a stop. Screaming . In a dead straight line. Right onto the hard shoulder. I can't believe my fuckin' luck. I get off. Shaklly. The chain has snapped. Wrapped itself around the back wheel. How the fuck did i survive that. My mates come back . The Motorway was empty in those days. They look. They can't believe my luck either. I don't think i'm gonna get too many chances like that i say. No they say. Probably not. We're still staring in disbelief. Stretching back up the road. A dead straight black skidmark. I sit and have a smoke.

I'm a bit shaky. We'll come back with the pick up they say. I sit there alone for half an hour. Staring. Looking at my hands shaking. They come back in an open landrover. With ramps. I think that's it for me and bikes i say. They don't say anything. Home.

We went to see U2 play The Milton Keynes Bowl with the bikers. My brother came down from London. With all his footballing mates. It pissed with rain all day. The Ramones and Spear of Destiny were support. They played real good. The Ramones seemed to play the entire 'It's Alive' LP as the rain came down in sheets, excellent. But... During a lull in the rain. One of my brothers mates, Brad, gets down from the bank and starts singing. 'Blue Heaven.' It's one they sing on the terraces. At Arsenal. All the rest sing along .Repeating every line. After two renditions he finishes. Half the Mk Bowl is Applauding. Cheering for more. He sings it again. Seems like the whole place is singing along – 'Just Molly and me,(just molly and me), And Baby Makes Three (and baby makes three) Living in my (living in my), Blue heaven' (blue heaven). The audience erupts. He takes a bow. More cheering. What a star. That was better than any of the bands i thought. I don't think i was the only one.

My brother moved to The States. He's going to be a soccer coach. In Atlanta. I wonder if he'll teach them how to fight on the terraces.
I had given up all my punk friends when i left town. Except for Tony. I couldn't face them. That whole place just reminded me of Suzy and punk.
So. One night in the village Pub. Just got my first car. It's a green golf 1600ls.1976. No more bikes for me. We all pile in at midnight. Drive down to town to the nearest nightclub. Never been in one before. Being a punk meant it wasn't a good idea. Still. Not a punk anymore. This feels better. Not standing out. Emma the beautiful disco dolly

comes too. We get to the club and we're in. Straight up to the bar. After a few more pints we're all dancing to Lulu singing 'Shout'. This place wasn't exactly classy. Suddenly it's half two in the morning. Emma's gone off with someone. Not me. It's time to go home. We all cram into the car. A police van and a squad car cruise past. Down to the club entrance. That's the way in & out of the carpark. Bollocks. Pissed up logic. I decide to go over the curb at the edge of the car park. Straight onto the road. Instead of going past the coppers at the entrance. Halfway over .The exhaust catches on the curb.There's a few too many people in it. Oh shit. It now sounds like a tractor. All my mates get out and run off. Nothing for it. I get out and crawl underneath. Trying to put the concertina section back into the pipe where it's ripped it out. I must be pissed. I can't believe it. It's gone in. Just as i finish i see a big pair of boots walking along the car. They stop next to me. A voice says 'Ello Ello, What's going on 'ere then'. Oh fuck. That's all i need. A copper with a sense of humour. I slide out from under the car. I look up into the face of my old childhood friend Geoff. Fuck me i say.You're a copper. Fuck me he says.You're pissed. Yes. I'm afraid i am. I tell him what happened. He asks who it was that ran off. I tell him they're the village lot. Some mates he says. Hmm. He asks if i can drive straight. I seem to have sobered up a bit. Yes i say. Hang on here then. He walks back across the car park to where the rest of the coppers are. Has a word. Comes back over. Tells me to get down onto the road and follow him. He'll take me out to the village turn. He pulls round in front of me. Sticks his blue flashing light on. He's laughing. Fuck me i can't believe my luck. I follow him out of town. We see my mates from the village walking home. Me and Geoff both beep our horns .Stick our fingers up at them as we pass. They don't know what's happening. Fuck 'em they can walk. Teach them to run off. I get to the village turn. Geoff stops.Gets out. Comes over. Asks if I'll be alright going up the lane ? Yes. Good. Don't do it again he says. Message received and understood captain. He tells me to Fuck off . Laughing. It's what we used to say to each other when we used to play 'Star Trek'. Thanks Geoff . I am a fuckin idiot . Yep, he says - ain't we all. Gets in his squad car and drives off back into town. I drive home. Up to the village. Bed. Could've been a cell.

Glastonbury

I started to go around with some of my brother's old mates. From Wolverton. These were different. Graduates mostly, who had decided to take more than just the one year off. They were having a damn good time.There was Fruit(who wasn't). Junior. Storky. Egg. Fatman(who wasn't) Silver Fox..The lovely Ripper. My friend Pigsy knocked around with them too. Loads of others. Have you ever been to Glastonbury they asked. No i said. Isn't that just for bikers? We're going. Come with us they said. Oh yes.

We drove down at four in the morning. in Storky's Vauxhall viva. Smoking joints listening to Roxy Music 'Like a Hurricane' live. The Shaggs singing 'My Pal Foot Foot' what the fuck is that ? It's so bad it's brilliant. I don't remember much else of that journey. I wasn't used to smoking .We were followed by Robin in his newly restored MG roadster. Scum on his big Suzuki. Pigsy on his yellow Honda 400 four. I don't remember how everyone else got there. We arrived. Fuck me it's like Mad Max. There's Hell's Angels. Other assorted biker gangs. Hippies. Students. This was before the giant fences. Before police were on site. They had an agreement. They'd just sit outside the entrance. Unless there was trouble. There wasn't any. Not really. Only about 35,000 people. I had never seen that many people in one place. For a party. I could not believe this could exist in England. There were people walking around with satchels. Shouting out 'Red Leb 15 a quarter, Whizz 10 pound a gramme' over and over. Like market traders. The market. Bloody

Hell. There's stalls for everything. Big blackboards. With lists of what they were selling. You have got to be fuckin' kidding. It's all drugs. White lightning £2.50. Samurai blotters £2.50. Red Leb £15 1/4. Black £20. Speed(good stuff) £10. It was every where you looked. They would sell you cans of beer as well. Kids in a sweetshop. We bought red leb. What are those white lightning things i asked. They laughed. It's acid they said. LSD. Where have you been hiding. Not at University i said. I started to feel that maybe i had missed out on something. I had never seen it before. We asked the biker. Are they any good. He asked if we'd ever done it before. Yes we said. These babies last a whole day he said. Are you sure you want them ?. You bet your sweet bippy we said. He laughed and handed us a small square of blotting paper each. With a japanese letter on them. Here we go then. I was nervous and excited. I couldn't fuckin' wait. I thought this stuff had disappeared. It was like a legend.

Half an hour later. Nothing. Hmm i thought. We been ripped off. We're sitting under a pylon on the hillside. There's someone playing with a sort of white bird thing that they were throwing to each other. Like a paper plane. I'm watching it glide between them. It is so beautiful. I turn to Storky. He's watching it too. Isn't that beautiful i say. Yes he says. Suddenly I feel very strange. Like i'm talking in slow motion. Everything feels so spacious. Bloody 'ell says Storky. Fuck's sake says Junior. Scum is just Grinning. From ear to ear. It feels like sitting in a strong wind. Without the wind. It's life you're feeling says Storky. Wow! He's right. That's what it is. Life coursing through me. It's everywhere. I see it in the air. In the grass. In the clouds. Those clouds. They're white and fluffy. Like little lambs. I can see one that looks like a lamb. It's jumping around the sky. I'm laughing. I'm laying on my back. I feel like i'm in a film set. Nothing feels real. Special effects. Everything has changed. I feel like i'm seeing the world for the first time. It is so wonderful. I say I can't speak.

Storky laughs . Yes you can he says. I can't quite understand how i'm doing it. I am losing my powers of conscious movement. I'm looking at my hands without quite remembering what they are. Come on says Fruit. Lets go for a walk. We all look at him like he's mad. Then we all get up and follow him. It's like my body is on automatic. My head feels wide open and cool. Hey Storky i say. I can't .I can't . I can't manage to say any more than that. He pats me on the back and tells me I'll be alright.

Off we go. Snow white and the seven dwarves. It feels like we're in a cartoon. There's a beautiful Hari Krishna girl trying to get Pigsy to say Krishna. How about a blowjob he says. They just keep repeating the same things. I think he should leave her alone. She thinks he should say Krishna. He thinks she should give him a blowjob. It all seems very complicated to me. Everyone looks weird as we walk past them. There's another Krishna girl. She looks awful familiar. I stare at her she smiles at me. Click. It's Poly Styrene. The singer from Xray Spex. 'Aren't you Poly Styrene?' I ask. 'I used to be' she said and laughed. Blimey. Vive le Punk.

It finally occurs to me that everyone else in the place are out of their heads too. That seems like a good thought. My stomach is butterflies. My eyes are ... i don't know what they are. Seeing. Breathing. Walking. It all seems so miraculous. I finally see how wonderful life is. And how small a part we play in this world. But it seems like the world loves us. All. Yes says Storky. It does. We are it's children. Did i say that out loud. I don't know says Storky. But i heard you somehow. Fuck me i thought. What is this stuff ? A present from God or something? I feel like i'm floating. I don't know how long we wandered around the site. Eventually we got back to our tents. Robin wasn't with us anymore. He had his girlfriend with him. We knew he'd be o.k. But his car was still here. Parked next to us. Uh-Oh. Fruit said wouldn't it be funny if we hid his car. Don't you think he might get upset i said. Oooh no said Fruit. We're starting to get the hang of this stuff. About five minutes and he had managed to find a key to open the door and the crooklok. Somehow. He started up and drove it slowly. About 100 yards. Parked it behind some other tents. It now seemed hilarious. We were all giggling. Lets go and watch a band said Junior. Blimey. I'd forgotten about the bands.

We get down to the main stage. Black Uhuru are just starting to play. We are sitting on the grass. At the back of the crowd. Bloody hell. They are heavy. They are very good. I have never seen a reggae band before. Wow. We notice that Pigsy is looking increasingly strange. Even to us. It is very hot and sunny. I turn to Pigsy. I tell him I'm so hot i could just about peel my skin off. It was supposed to be funny. He didn't think so. He gibbered something unintelligible. Then he gets up and runs off into the crowd. Everyone else is howling with laughter. Quick says Fruit. Run the other way. That's what we do. All laughing. It's like hide and seek.

I can't quite seem to remember what my watch is supposed to tell me. I'm looking at it and it means nothing. I ask Egg what it's for . He dissolves into a helpless fit of giggles. Doubled up on the grass. Who cares . Not me. Then Egg gets up and pisses on Fruits leg. Just like that. He's laughing out loud now. So are we. Fruit isn't. But Egg is one big musclebound thug. Fruit isn't.

I don't know what bands we saw after that. We made our way back up the hill. There's a Hari Krishna tent. We go in. It's a free food tent. Oh yeah. I'd forgotten about eating. We get some food. It tastes good. We are still completely off our trolleys. Get a chair says junior. What for i ask. We'll have a bonfire he says. We can't do that i said. Oh yes we can. Just take one. They're folding wooden ones. I take one. We all do. The Hari Krishnas just smile at us. What the fuck is going on . 'Glastonbury' says Fatman. 'It's great isn't it'. Yeah. Sure is.

Back by the tents. The bonfire looks great. We're drinking Scrumpy and staring into the flames. Smoking Rocky Gold. Robin found his car and drove home with the hump. He didn't think it was very funny. That made it even funnier. We laughed at him as he drove off . Tripping. All the way back to M.K. in the dark. Blimey.

Much later. A figure comes stumbling into the firelight. Sweating. A face of fear. He's crying. It's Pigsy. He's been gone hours. He's sitting in the fire. We pull him out. I'm not sure how many hours passed but he finally manages to speak. He said he fell over down near the front of the crowd. He looked up and saw three giant Rastas staring down at him. He said they were a hundred foot tall. He Freaked.Then he took off. Flew up into the sky he said. He looked down from on high. Shouted at himself to run away. He kept shouting it. Eventually the giants left him alone. He dropped down and fell into a yellow sea. He was drowning in it . Trying to swim . Someone had picked him up at that point. It wasn't a yellow sea. It was his biker jacket. Yellow to match his Bike. He didn't seem to be coping with it all very well.

What seemed like weeks later i'm leaning against Storky's car. I'm talking to Ripper. She's indian. Bollywood babe. I can't seem to string a sentence together. I wish i could. She's beautiful. When's this stuff going to stop i ask. Fuckin' ell. It's been 14 hours.

All i remember about the rest of the weekend is smoking dope. Seeing 'The Funboy Three' doing the Doors song 'The end'. Terry Hall waving a flaming American Flag whilst singing it. In the dark. Wow.....

Onwards

I thought about it. I signed up for 6th Form College. As a mature student. What me ? You've got to be having a laugh. Off i went. After a few weeks i made some friends. What a bunch. There was Dj Picci. Gordon. Dylan and Jo Bombshell. Funky Colin and Daz. Matty and Hann. Blimey she's beautiful. Loads of others. All into music. We go and see Cabaret Voltaire. They were having fun. I needed it. This is great. Sixth form was just like school though. Tossers telling me what to do. Fuck 'em. What did they know. They'd never left school. How butch. Rebel without a brain me.

I met this French guy. Francis. He's from Bordeaux. He's an assistant teacher .Over here for a year or so. He's into music. We get on great. He's lodging with another teacher. She's got loads of cats. The house stinks. We all go around together. Some of them know Storky and co. from Wolverton. What a gang.

They had a group. Ha Ha Guru. Sort of cross between Psychedelic Small Faces and Japan. Fruit sang the Dave Sylvain vocals. Storky did the cheeky chappie stuff. Fatman played keyboards. They played at the Joint. They were great. More of a studio band really though. That's where Storky worked. He had access to all the studio toys. Their tapes were great. Flugal horns. German Ooompah music. Bongoes and guitars. Trippy stuff. Fancy that.

A couple of months later. Me and Storky got some acid. Pink Panthers. We went out in Wolverton. To a pub. I was driving my Golf. The trip came on in the pub. This is too much I say. It is. Fuckin' ell. Alright he says. Out we go to the car. Storky I say. I can't drive. Yeah you can just sit here for a few minutes. I'm not sure if I'm dreaming. It's not that strong but it's a job to think properly. I put on the cassette. It's Mike Bloomfield Steve Stills and Al Kooper. 'Super Session'. Oh for fuck's sake. That guitar. Storky's laughing. So am i. A friend of mine bought me that L.P. for my 9th Birthday. Didn't like it then, it wasn't Slade or Trex. I sure liked it now. The tape I'd made for the car must have been full of crackles and hisses. Didn't notice any though. It's coming on with a vengeance. I open my door. Sit with my legs out. In the car park. The car stereo sounds like nothing I've ever heard. How can it sound like that. It's only two tinny little door speakers. Storky says that is fuckin'incredible. He's right it is. We sit there until the tape stops. 45 minutes. Wow. That is definitely some guitar. Lets go to a gig says Storky. OK. I'm driving. Everything seems slowww. I look from the speedo to the mirror. Mirror to the speedo. Oooh yes . Musn't forget the road as well. Slight paranoia. Fuck . There's a police car coming the other way. It's ok says Storky you're doing fine. They don't know you're tripping. Oh bloody hell. Of course they don't. Mellow out man. I start to giggle. My car feels like a cartoon car. I know that if we crash it'll hurt though. I'm being careful. It's like steering a sail boat. We get to the gig. It's upstairs in a pub. Storky asks if I can play. Yeah course I can I say. Up we get. Storky starts a 12 bar on the keyboard. I'm stood there with the guitar. I'm looking at it. Oh shit. What is this thing. I cannot remember a single note. People start to look at me. Uh-oh. Then, fuck me. The lights all go out. What's going on. Storky's laughing. I think I can see in the dark. Power cut he says. Thank fuck for that . I'm sorry I just couldn't remember how to play. Don't worry he says you were great. People are lighting candles. We go downstairs into the pub .Everywhere is lit with candles. It's like the olden days. There's people I know in there. They try to speak to me. I can't speak. This is too much. We have a drink and make an exit. I cannot remember where we went after that . Or where I woke up.

Some weeks later. Storky says there's an all night horror thing at Bletchley Cinema. Oh Goody. Acid. Nightmare on Elm Street. The Excorcist. Don't remember what the other ones were. My little sister came too. I think she likes one of Storky's friends. We spent the night giggling. My little sister didn't know what was going on. Couldn't exactly tell her we were tripping. By the end of the night we were tired out from laughing so much. She was terrified . Didn't you think they were scary she said. No . They were great. Oh dear. Not a good example.
Have you read Carlos Castenada ? asks Storky. I haven't. What about Tom Woolf's 'Electric kool aid acid test', Jay Stevens 'Storming Heaven' ? He gives me them. Wow. I read them over and over. I knew there was more to life. Here it all was. In print. Week nights i'm lost in the Mexican desert and sixties California. I'm hooked.

Big Wide World

Me and Francis. Got a flat. At the YMCA Milton Keynes. It takes all day to move in. It's 7 in the evening. We've been here three days. Someone knocks at the door. It's two girls. Ones got black and white dyed hair. New Romantic.They're wearing baby doll nighties. They're wearing furry kitten heel slippers and feather boa's. Honestly. They've got a bottle of champagne. They're our welcoming committee they say. Blimey. They come in. Francis has got The Sisters of Mercy playing on the stereo. We smoke red leb. We drink champagne. We go to bed. So this is Milton Keynes. It's great. It's mad.

A night out at 'The Joint' club. With my friends Douggie and Neeta. All the college lot are there. And Storky and co. And Tony. It's new romantic. It's punk. Alien Sex Fiend are playing a concert. I think they look like the New York Dolls. We're speeding off our heads. Pink Novocaine. It's clean. Not like Sulphate. From our Scouse friend. It's heaven. He gets good stuff. Two a.m. Club shuts. We go for a drive. In Douggies Lotus. It's a 1969 Elan convertible. It's beautiful. It should be. He's just finished a nut & bolt restoration. Blue over white. Gold Stripe. It's a warm summer night. Down the dual carriageway. What the fuck is that. It's a naked man. Thumbing a lift. It's Mark. One of the transvestites from the club. Like Pete Burns. He's naked except for his black stilletto boots. He's six foot plus. We stop. He's speeding. He's not scared. He says it's ok. He's just trying to pick up a man. We leave him . We're laughing. We see him the next week. He said he pulled . A really nice builder he said. This place is crazy.

Back to the flat. Big Bernard opens the door. He's French. He's staying with us. He just came out of Jail in France for armed robbery. His passport doesn't say Bernard. He can get them. They're very good. He's covered in blood. Fuck. Where's Francis. Don't go in the kitchen says Bernard. Francis is in there. I see blood on the floor. Fuck. I go in the kitchen. There's blood on the walls. There's blood on the floor. It's everywhere. Fuck. Francis is leaning over the sink. Fuck. He turns around. I see it. It's a fuckin' stag. A whole one. I couldn't believe it. They'd been to a concert in Bedford. They'd hit it coming back through Woburn park. And brought it home. Tied across the top of his Renault five.They hadn't seen any coppers he said. I laughed. They laughed. He butchered it. In our kitchen. Him and big Bernard. Johnny Thunders was singing 'You can't put your arms around a memory' whilst they did it. We ate venison. For a week.. The food of kings. The bin cupboard was under the flats. They put the remains in there. Two black bin bags full. One had the pair of antlers sticking out of the top. They stayed there for six days. The binmen took them. No one said a word. Yep. This place is crazy.

We all went on days out. Boating on the river in Cambridge. Stoned out of our heads. Going into peoples private gardens. Floating past them as they picnicced. Eating in a Jamaican Restaurant run by some hippies in the back room of a shop. Giant paper globe lampshades that I just stare at.

All sorts of fun. Bernard finally went home. After a couple of months

Francis moved back to France at the end of the year. I was sorry to see him go. It had been great. I'd made a friend there. He had a good leaving party though. People shagging in the bath. Shaving off Egg's quiff while he was out for the count. Drawing on his face with a marker pen. Fruit's brother shaved off all fruits pubes. He never even woke up. Some of us wandered over the road. To the information tent. A giant inflatable room. Like a bouncy castle. But bigger. We climbed up it to the top.About twenty feet. Then we slid down. What a ride. After ten minutes or so the coppers turned up. Get down they shouted. No we shouted. Come and get us. They went away in the end. Not very happy. We were. We thought it was hilarious. As you would. Being stoned. Ho ho ho. The flat got trashed. There were about 15 people crashed out in the end. Bit of a mess in the morning. Never mind we were giving back the keys later on.

New City

Me and the Scouser. Go to see Gary Glitter play at Aylesbury. He's got a MK 3 Cortina. Red with a black vinyl roof. Bucket seats. Skull gearknob. It is cool. He's got Novocaine. Clean. Numb. Not anxious and sweaty like speed. We spend the entire journey talking. The support is the original Glitter Band. Singing along to 'Let's get together again'. I think apart from that we spent the entire gig talking. Babbling. Noone said anything to us. He does look very heavy. He is. What a fast night.

I bought a car from one of the bikers. It's a red sharknose '73 Chevy Camaro. Excellent.
I moved in with the Scouser. He was a Biker. His girlfriend lived there too. And his sister. Black and blue spiky hair. Studded leather jacket. Fishnets. She was a Gothic Punk. I thought she was gorgeous. She thought i was a flash twat. I had a yank motor. I was her brother's friend. I sold drugs. We knew each other from The Joint nightclub. I never felt flash. I was running on empty They played Fleetwood Mac's 'Tusk'. Frank Zappa. The Cult. Lloyd Cole's 'Rattlesnakes.' I played Elvis.Tom Waits. Hawkwind. Yello. The Rocky Horror Soundtrack. Motown. The record player was on all the time. This was fun. He parked his Honda 750 four in the front room. Rode it in up the front steps. He drove a Sweeney Granada now. Biker Goth. That was some house. Seemed like we were speeding all the time. Nice stuff. They were great.

One night in the pub. I'm tripping. Off my head. Completely flying. I'm sitting talking slowly to her at a little table. Vision are singing 'Lucifer's Friend'. It seems like a dream to me. I'm looking at my hands whilst i'm talking. They are amazing me. I just keep turning them over. Suddenly she gets up. Walks off. What did i do. I'm looking after her longingly. I can't get up. Malc comes over. He said I freaked her out. You were answering her questions before she had asked them. Can you read minds he asks. Fuckin' ell. I don't know. We get back to the house. We're all sitting in the front room. She's looking at me. She's playing Paul and Paula's 'Hey Paula'. Look i say. Pointing to a big print on the wall. As i point it falls to the floor with a crash. Fuck's sake. She runs upstairs to her room. Shuts the door. How the fuck did you do that asks Malc. I don't know. This is getting weird. Malc says I'm fuckin ' crazy. I think he might be right. But we all saw it.

There's some 5 minute religious thing on the tele. Before it closes at midnight. A priest comes on and just stares at the screen. We all look . Waiting for him to say something. Five minutes and he hasn't said a word. We start looking at each other. What the fuck's going on. After what seems like hours he says 'your eyes are doves'. Stares knowingly out of the screen and it's over .The screen goes blank. We are stunned into silence. We sit and listen to some of Malc's records; Ella Fitzgerald singing 'I wonder Why', Dean Martin singing 'Little Old Wine Drinker Me'. Excellent stuff.

We try and work out what he means. It's very difficult when you're tripping. It becomes a catchphrase for us. When we're pissed off in the week. Waiting for the weekend – 'Remember, your eyes are doves'. Usually does the trick. Giggles all round. Even adverts seem to take on new meanings when you're tripping. There's one for fairy liquid. 'It's all greasy auntie. – Jenny! – She's right you know'! Everything on tele seems hilarious. We never seem to watch it when we're straight though.

We went for midnight walks. Tripping out of our heads. Around the new city. It wasn't finished. There were loads of fields not built on yet . Between the city centre and the house. Roads that just stopped. Eddie Stanton's 'Milton Keynes We Love you, Like fuck we do'. How good was that song. Very. We lived those lyrics. 'How can people find their way, when the roads don't go nowhere ?' It was still dark out there. None of the streetlights were connected. We walked for miles sometimes. Climbing up an unfinished office block. Staring out across the half lit cityscape. There's just floors and pillars. No outside walls. Im leaning off the edge. Hanging onto one of the concrete reinforcing posts. Singing the doors L.A Woman -'City at night, City at night'. At the top of my voice. Well. I think it's funny. The post bends. I'm staring out into nothing. I'm hanging 60 feet off the ground. Fuck. Malc grabs me round the waist. We fall back in. Laughing. Yeah Baby.... Every step seemed like an adventure. We went down into the roundabout on the dual carriageway. It had just been planted with trees. It was like a little forest. We sat in there for hours. Watching the cars trailing. Giggling. Feeling like the famous five. Except I don't think they did Acid.

Sometimes when we got home we bumped into the milkman. We knew him from the pub. He lived opposite. He was only young. Some nights he'd come over and get stoned. Then we'd all hop on his milkfloat and go delivering the milk with him. Tripping. Now that was fun. The Scouser would go off to work. Don't know how he did it. He welded the frames for the new buildings. Thirty feet up in a harness. A city built on partying. He was hardcore. Mr.non stop. Sometimes me and Malc would go and wait for the 7 – 11 to open. Cans of Red Stripe for breakfast. Then hit the café for a fry up. Lose the rest of the waking hours in dreamland. The curtains were always shut in that house.

I had a job in the week. Working for my dad. He had an electronics company in M.K. there were people there I had known since I was little. It was a happy little family. Straight. I mentioned The Rocky Horror Show was playing on stage in London. The apprentices were up for it. We dressed up. Make up. Fishnets. Basques. Drove down to London. Walking down Wimbledon High

St. Getting wolf whistled at by blokes outside a pub. I cracked my bullwhip at them. Laughed back. It was a great night. Seemed like old times. Stopping off at the motorway services on the way back 2 in the morning. Got us some funny looks.

After a couple of years I left my job to do landscaping. Seemed like a good idea at the time. More flexibility, which was getting awful handy. Never was gonna be a shining example of the bosses son. I Had a friend on the MKDC. Got some nice contracts. OAP lawns. Grass verges along those dual carriageways. Tractor and mower heaven. Village stuff. I still kept in touch with some of my old workmates though. Still visited the factory.
Some of them came to a party at the house. It was packed. We even had the bouncers from the pub. People inside ,outside, over the road. Everyone was tripping. We gave it out for free. Some of them had a good time. Some didn't. One of them lying outside in the gutter looking at a puddle. Going on about being in a swimming pool. Oh dear. When world's collide.

London

My brother rings up. He's come back to England for a holiday. His mate Brad's having a leaving do. At his house in Enfield. Bring whoever you like he says. Okey doke. So. Me. Malc. Paul. Off down the M1 to meet them in a pub. It's in Islington. By the time we get there they're ready to go. Follow us they say. Jumping into their M.G. That's easy for them to say. They're not tripping. So. Speeding across London. Trying to follow their car. Through endless road works. Bloody cones. The Chevy is a bit big for slalom. It's like a spaceship dodging stars. We're all giggling. Finally we arrive. Tumbling out onto the verge. Laughing. You want to take it easy on those things says my brother. Yeah i say i know. We go in. There's Brad. One wall of the front room is covered by stacked up beer. I've never seen so many cans. They all seem very quiet. Mind you they're not tripping. We only did half. Didn't want to embarrass my brother. We start to talk to people. They all seem really nice. There's one guy. Just married. His wife's a real babe. Brad starts to sing 'Blue Heaven. After a bit of persuasion. Everyone joins in. Us too. Suddenly a piece of cake flies past his ear. Splats on the wall. That's it . Everyone starts. We're sitting quietly in front of the beer mountain. There's food flying everywhere. People cheering. So much for quiet. It seems to go on for ages. I think it did. When it stops there is food everywhere. Everyone's laughing like drains. We are amazed. People start to drift off. Brad dishes out sleeping bags. Dissappears upstairs. We're all lying in a line. Still quietly drinking beer. Next to me is Malc.

On the other side is the newlyweds. They seem to be getting awfully amorous. I turn away. Pass us a beer mate says the guy. I turn back around. His wife is sitting on top of him. Shagging him like there's no tomorrow. She sure is fit. I am speechless. He just laughs. Great ain't she he says. Sure is i say. I can see why you married her. He laughs and turns back to business. We still don't know what to do. So we roll over and finally go to sleep. Blimey. Londoners.

Pays de Galles

Malc met this girl. What a little honey. They got married. Just like that. We went to the wedding. What a day. Church and everything. Lovely. Couldn't really see myself following suit anytime soon though. Shame.

Me, Emma the Disco Dolly, Funky Colin and Daz ended up at a very weird party afterwards. After taking a cab and discussing loudly how we were going to get out and run. Paid in the end though. The cab driver looked relieved. So was i. Emma the disco dolly was getting people to sniff a jar of Marmite. They were so off their heads they thought it was drugs of some sort. Mind you, there was a lot of stuff going round. Made me giggle.

Malc and his lady moved to North Wales. They bought a farm. We said we'd visit soon. The summer just seemed to disappear.

Finally we get around to it....Half a gramme of whizz. All in one line. Each. Our poor noses. That stung like a bastard. Just to set us up for the drive . It was Christmas 1985. Off to the Llynn Peninsula in deepest Snowdonia. A different country. Escape. A Bag full of trips, black bombers, more whizz, Red Lebanese. Cans of Red Stripe. Two trays full. Five of us in the car. we were ready. We took the A5 all the way up to Shrewsbury. Stereo from the flat rigged up on the parcel shelf. Blasting out Yello's 'One second' and Hawkwind endlessly playing 'Space Ritual'. That was one fasssst Chevy ride. Seemed like minutes. All talking a hundred miles an hour. Stopped at the Five Horseshoes in Shrewsbury. For food. For more beers. Next part of the journey through Snowdonia National Park. In the dark. In the frost. Drunk and drugged up. Mmmm.

Two hours in. The thought finally hit. We're lost. Oh fuck. It's very dark here. It's not like the city. More by luck than judgement, a village. Halle-fuckin-lujah. Through the sleet a copper stood by a roundabout. In a rainsmock. I stopped. I rolled down the window. 'Excuse me...' It was wet outside. He stuck his head in. 'Lost are you boys'? Two Spliffs going. All of us with cans of Stripe. We told him where we were headed. Was it me or was he smiling? Fuck, what did i do that for? He gave us directions. He reached across me and took Paul's spliff. 'Not thinking of moving here are you boys'? NO ,we said in unison. We stared at his uniform. We couldn't move. Jo coughed. I held my breath. 'Good. If you lay off this you might find it quicker boyo' He took my can from between my knees. He took a long drag from the spliff. He drained the can in one go. He roared with laughter.'Night night boys, drive careful now.' He walked off back into the gloom. We sat there. In silence. We started to giggle. We laughed. We roared. We got out of the car. We couldn't speak we were laughing so hard. We leaned on the car. Five minutes. We got soaked. We didn't feel the cold. In and off again. Exiting the village, The copper just walking up his driveway. I had one of those horns that played Colonel Bogie, like the Dukes of Hazzard. It suited the Chevy. I gave him a blast. He slapped his knees with laughter. We waved. Welcome to Wales.

Finally arrived at The Farm at 0400. We got lost - Again. Look through the window. Malc hasn't answered the door. He's asleep. Sprawled out on the floor. He's still holding a half empty bottle of Jack Daniels. Bollocks. His drinking seems to have got worse since moving to the middle of nowhere. What was funny once just didn't seem it now. He's married. What the fuck is he playing at ? Finally we managed to wake him. I think we nearly broke the front door. We gave him a big line. He perked up. Tom Waits on his stereo - 'In The Neighbourhood'. We'd bought everything for Christmas dinner in the boot. He perked up some more. His wife came home. She was a diamond. We missed them. They cooked the food. 1000. Still speeding. We ate Christmas Dinner. It tasted wonderful. We had Champagne. We had cocaine. We had Red Stripe. We watched a 'Doors' video. Then we all slept a whole day. Happy Christmas? You better believe it baby.

Boxing day. The phone goes. It's Suzy. Jesus. She got the number from my mum. She says happy christmas. I don't know what to say to her anymore. I just say goodbye. Where do I have to go to escape ? Why do i keep finding things and people to escape from ?

We go outside. It was sunny. it was cold. It wasn't windy. We wrapped up. We walked along the coastal path to Hells Mouth. We had Red Stripe, we had spliffs. We had taken acid. For a change. Everything was black and white. Like someone had turned the colour down. We sat and watched the sea and the winter sun for an eternity. Looking across towards Anglesey. The sea was flat as a millpond. I held Jo's hand. She held mine. All day. Finally it started to get dark. We floated back to the farm. - Wow man. We went to the nearest off licence. It was five miles away. We bought trays of beer. We bought Champagne. We bought Vodka. We bought Cigarrettes. We almost cleaned the place out. The boot of the car was full. The owner laughed. We laughed. She would close early she said. Happy Christmas we said. Ho Ho Ho.

Gone

My brother's back from America again. I pick him up in the Chevy. The irony is not lost. He had a new one in the states. I only got 'Second hand wings full of patches'. Like Hoyt Axton. Never mind. Dire Straits are the biggest band on the planet at the moment. I've got two tickets for their show at the NEC. And a coach ride there and back. 'Brothers in arms', The Cult's album 'Love', Yello's '80 - 85 In One Go'. Playing those babies to death at the moment. Non Stop.It's 1985. What a show. Didn't hear a bad note all night. They sure can play guitar. I'm getting into a lot of old 60's music. It's like there's something in there. A message for me. Waiting. I wonder if i'm starting to lose it.

It's all starting to get a bit heavy. It didn't start out like this. I just knew someone who could get acid. Lots of it. And speed lots of it. Fuckin Kilos. It was Tony. We had Supermen, We had Omms We had Pink Panthers, We had White lightning. We had whatever we wanted. It was like christmas. Every week. Tony knew people everywhere. He'd been travelling. He'd been to India. He'd been to Amsterdam. He'd been to Germany. I'd stayed . I knew everyone here. Word spreads fast. Milton Keynes was still a new city. Sprung out of the fields like some wild west frontier town. It was wide open.It wasn't Leighton. Tony was happy for me to be the man. It kept him a secret. He networked. Abroad. He didn't need to shout to make himself heard. People listened to him. Chairman Tone .

There were Gangs of builders from up north. They lived in on site. Two months at a time.They were building the city. They liked to work fast. I sold speed like there was no tomorrow. Fuckin Pounds of it. It was never ending. It ended for Jock the builder. He was caught in a pub car park . Boot full of Speed. He got ten years. Don't bring your shit down here and try and undercut us. We don't like it. Turns out it was only 19 percent pure. Bastard. They didn't mind him going inside. He was selling poor quality. If there's another time we'll put them under the new Dual carriageway. Our builders work it on nights. We can bury anything we like. It's all getting a bit heavy.

Two years of work. Me and Tony. Big Steve was our introduction. He was from here. He knew everyone we didn't. He was ten years older than us. We knew him from boxing club. Since we were 11 years old. He had a vicious temper. Soulboy Steve. Been chucked out of the A.B.A. for fighting someone in the audience. Before a match. He was going up to Wigan Casino when we were still in shorts. In his Loon pants and cap sleeves. An Addidas holdall full of uppers. To sell. He was the man. He never got into punk. We were out of it. Now we were all - we were all - just in it together. Music's music, everyone likes soul anyway don't they? I do. Trust was not a problem between us three. Sorcerer's apprentice me. We got our gear out of Liverpool. It came from Amsterdam. Straight in. No problem.

Friday. After i'd made the drop. Back to the house. Laying on the floor in the front room. Frank Zappa on the stereo. I'm tripping. Two supermen . They're strong. I'm seeing colours. I seem to have lost the power of speech. I can't remember how to form words. I can't remember who i am. That's the point. I have failed at everything i've ever done. I am good at this. I am the fuckin' man. It's my choice. It'll probably kill me. That's the point. Way to go. I sell between one and two thousand trips a week. every week. I send some down to my friends in Brighton. Through the post.I hear The Zap Club is really swinging down there at weekends. I'll have to go for a night out sometime. Never seem to find the time. Steve's crew sells a thousand of them on into London. They are old hands at this game. I sell a kilo of speed a month. Sometimes i sell black bombers. Not many. A couple of hundred maybe. For give aways at parties, i get Dexedrine. I buy them in bags of a thousand. From my friend the chicken farmer. It's not all Townie shit. They feed them to the chickens to keep them awake and lay more eggs. Poor fuckers. I must remember not to eat eggs. Chicken Dexy's.They are four for a pound. Cheap as sweets. I still make a profit. It's spiralling out of my control. It's all getting too big.

We know the head of the drug squad. Sort of. It's a long story. Actually we know his son. He went to boxing club too. That fucker owes us big time. He liked to think he was as bad as us. He wasn't. He didn't know the right people. Everyone knew his dad was a copper. He didn't have a deathwish. We owned him. We know when the busts are coming. It is the wild west. Here's how:

He smoked too much dope. In the daytime. Twat. One Saturday morning he got very very stoned. At his dad's house. His dad was away for the weekend. He thought it would be funny to go for a ride in his dad's brand new Opel Senator squad car. He went for a drive. He came to our place. What the fuck do you think you're doing. Bringing that thing here.You stupid cunt. We told him to fuck off. He fucked off. He was very stoned. He put it in a ditch. Now he was very stoned and very scared. He phoned us. A light bulb went on in my head. Steve . He said yes. He said straight away. Five minutes and he's there with his breakdown truck. It's starting to get dark. He's got hip hop blaring out of the window. Some group shouting 'Jive assed motherfuckers' over backing tracks. I think it's scary. It's violent. It sure isn't Nancy & Lee. We winch the Senator on the back. The copper's son is crying. What am i gonna do now he wails. My dad'll kill me. No says Steve. I've got a better idea. He pulls out a Polaroid camera. One instant photo of the copper's son, stood crying next to his old man's Senator. Oh Goody...

We pull in to Steve's Uncle's scrapyard. There's his uncle and one of his friends waiting. Right says Steve. Right says his uncle. Hmmm says his friend. His uncle gives out sledhgehammers. They start. Every panel. Every light. Every Window. They do not pause for breath. They have a sneer on their faces. Steve's screaming 'Cunts' as he swings his hammer. It is fuckin' terrifying . Disney's 'King of the Swingers' is now blasting out of

Steve's truck. Oh for fuck's sake. They stop. The car is trashed. If it could bleed it would. To death. Hold on says Steve. He's not finished yet. He gets his cock out. He walks around the car. Pissing all over it. Right he says. His uncle drops the grab onto it. Crunch it goes. Into the crusher. Steve and his friend spit at it as the jaws close. It's gone. They do not have smiles on their faces. They kick the side of the crusher. They stand there staring at it. It is not a nice look. Their relationship with the police is not a good one. Steve's dad died in police custody when he was eight. He'd been a robber. In London. We drop off the coppers son. It's only three hours later. He now knows nothing about his dad's car.

He never even heard it being driven off. Must have been during the night he said. We now have that polaroid. His dad keeps written files. At home. The computer age is still young. Oh goody. So there. Make the connection. Everyone grew up somewhere. I know everyone round here. People like me. I always remember. It's starting to eat into my life.

Breather

Queen are playing at Knebworth. With Status Quo. Now that sounds like a good day out. I ask everybody. Steve. The bikers from the village pub. We all decide to go. Oh goody. I know they're not maybe the trendiest thing to like. Good music goes above all that though. Queen certainly are that. Entertainers extrordinaire. After all we've all grown up listening to them. Even Quo. Not everything has to be about fashion. Good times are good times.

Drive up to the village pub. In my new toy. I've bought a beach buggy. It's great. There's a big row of bikes parked outside. Gleaming. The bikers are sitting on the Patio drinking Red Stripe. The windows are open. Rainbow's 'Since you been gone' blasting out. Sun shining. Excellent. I get myself a pint. Five minutes later. Steve and his gang turn up. He's got a Triumph Stag. Very 70's cool. Two of his mates sat up on the rear. One in the front. Oh bugger.I never thought about a problem between bikers and soulboys. They're all my friends. I see some hard stares as they all get out though. I go to the bikers and explain. These are good friends of mine. Come for a good day out with us. Steve's stood behind me. No problem son he says. Let's party. Smiles break out. Rush's 'The Spirit of Radio' is blasting out now. Good guitar. The atmosphere has got better. They're all talking. Thank fuck for that. It would've been a kind of long day otherwise. Finally we're off. The landlord comes out to wave us off. Jefferson Starship's 'Jane' is halfway through. Ten ten . We've got ourselves a convoy. Wahoo !

The cruise up there was great. I've got Sam Cooke's greatest hits on my stereo. He sure can sing. We all park up and get in just as the Quo start. We get some drinks and go and sit up on the hill .Just back from the front. After a couple of pints we head towards the front. They're doing 'Rockin' all over the world'. Seems like everyone is smiling. This is great. I don't remember what order thay played what. I do remember everyone singing and clapping along to 'Sweet Caroline ' though. A bunch of Soulboys ? Blimey. Quo were great.

Then Queen. The band are playing . It's dark. Suddenly there's Freddie. Atop a giant double staircase. He's wearing an Ermine gown. And a crown. He's punching the air. So are the thousands in the audience. He shouts something .Can't hear what but that's it. They've started. Wow ! I stood spellbound for the entire set. I can't explain it. That was just the best thing i have ever seen. And i've seen a few. Absoloutely incredible. What a showman. It was one of those things for me. I don't think i was alone. Everyone seemed to be thinking the same.And to know all the words. Like i did.

We left. The bikers sped off. Back to the village ASAP for some after hours drinking. I cruise home in the buggy. I come off the main road. Turn up towards the village. There's smoke everywhere. I can see flames here and there. All along both sides of the road. Blimey. What's going on ?

They're burning stubble. I'd forgotten about that. Have i been away that long? Feels like a lifetime ago that i was a village boy. It looks medieval or something. I suppose it looked the same then. Bloody great. I pull off the road through an open gate. Park on the edge and sit there looking at it smoking a fag. Through gaps i can see how far it goes on. Bloody miles it looks like. I'm sitting there humming 'Are you lonesome tonight'. Out of the smoke a figure looms. It's one of the farmers from the village. Oh it's you he says. He's got two rabbits dangling over his shoulder. A 12 Bore in his hand. Look he says. Smoked rabbit. He collapses in fits of laughter. So do i. Silly fucker. He asked me what I was up to . I just want to look for a bit if that's alright. OK he says. But don't be doing any rabbit impersonations . Tells me I'm a nutter . I know i say. I know. Fuckin tell me about it. He walks off into the smoke laughing. I just want to remember this day. Get it fixed in my mind. A whole adventure. No drugs .We didn't do them in the daytime. We weren't junkies. I think i just wanted to remind myself of that. I sat there smoking and looking out across the fields for a couple of hours. Thinking. About Elvis. Who the fuck am i. I'm not a city boy. Not really a villager anymore. Square peg in a round hole. I feel i'm drifting through life. Lost. I'm thinking about Don Juan. Choose a path with heart he said. It's a job to see one through all this smoke. I've got that phrase tattooed on my chest. In French. 'Choisir le chemin avec coeur'. Much later I cruised back up to the village .It's not easy driving quietly in a beach buggy. With an unsilenced VW engine. But i did my best. Bed. I fall asleep listening to Meat Loaf.

Zoom

A week or two later. I'm driving to Tony's. In the buggy. I've got a grand in my pocket. And 500 trips. I come up to the new round about. There's nothing planted on it yet. Just a curb. I look in my rear view mirror. There's something zooming up behind me. Ha ha. Want a race ? Watch this. I drop a gear and floor it. I jump straight over it. Now there's a flashing blue light in my mirror. Oh fuck. I pull over. Not much choice really. A copper walks up. I get out. He's laughing. It's fuckin' Geoff. I don't believe it. He's shaking his head. What the fuckin' ell was that he says. I tell him I'm sorry. I didn't see it was a cop car. I guessed that he said. Is it yours . Is it all legal ? .Yes . Tell me you're not pissed this time he says. No . Well i'm gonna have to do you for something he says. My Colleague wasn't very impressed. He walks around it. Gets his pad out. Writes me a ticket for exceeding 30 miles an hour. And something to present my documents at the station. Now he says .Fuck Off and don't do it again. And don't give me that Star Trek shit you bastard. He's still laughing. Go on then. And drive round roundabouts if you can manage that. That is not a Starship. Yes sir Captain i say as i jump in. He sticks 2 fingers up at me as i roar off. Fuckin' ell. I always thought I had a guardian angel. Never thought it would be dressed up as a copper though.......

One week later. I'm with Tony. Driving to the City Centre. In the Chevy. Carefully. Something cruises past us. What the fuck is that. I cannot believe my eyes. It's a giant brontosaurus skeleton. Doing sixty miles an hour up the dual carriageway. It passes. Tony says it's 'The Mutoid Waste Company'. They make giant sculptures from rubbish he says.They've come to town. His mate Ian is Driving it. We follow them to the centre. They park outside the YMCA. Get out and walk over.They're staying for a week. It's Tuesday. We ask them if they fancy a party . We'll get the acid. And the sounds. You're on they say. Fancy a ride ? It's a long lorry chassis and running gear. With this Skeleton thing sculpted on top. It looks like nothing i've ever seen. We cruise around the city centre. Lots of looks. Some people look scared. Like they're afraid it might bite. This is so cool.

Saturday. We've spent the whole week calling people. From all over. The Mutoids have camped down by Caldecotte lake. There's no estates finished down there yet. Just building sites. They've been scouring them for rubbish . They've made all these giant sculptures from all the old pipes and stuff they found. Weird is not the word. The encampment looks like something from a Sci-Fi nightmare. That's in the daytime. Straight. We set up the sound system. Fuck me it's loud. Still there's no-one to annoy round here. They're looking at my car. How do you fancy a row of red shark fins. Front to back across the bonnet roof and boot they ask. They're not kidding. I'll see i say. All of a sudden it's evening. People start turning up. Hundreds of them. Big Steve and the Trendies from the nightclubs.There's my Scouse friends. All the local Goths. Hannah and Matt. Rita and Sharon. Babes. My little sister and her friends. Blimey there's Steve Spon from UKDecay with the Luton Lot. Some of the Leighton lot. Seems like everyone's here. Uncle Tom bleedin'

Cobley and all. The music's really going some. Toots and the Maytals. Ska Music blasting loud. The sound system's in a big marquee. Don't know where that came from. Down by the speakers there's Mutoid Ian. He's dancing with his arms stretched out. Like he's flying. I guess he is. Good Acid he says. Thanks . Good show we say. It is good acid. We're all tripping. Hundreds of us. This place looks surreal in the dark. The night goes crazy. There's so many people here. Some Gypsies start fighting with tent poles. From the marquee. We invited them. They buy loads of acid from us now. They used to sell crap microdots. Not anymore. Noone really gets hurt. They're all too out of their heads.

We go for a burn around the lake on the skull bus. About 20 of us. Hanging off the sides like a troop carrier. Ian's tripping off his head. Driving it. How can you do four wheel drifts on the grass in a lorry ? Me. Douggie & Neeta. Mattie and Paul the photographer. Tony & Spon. Don't know who else. I get convinced he's going into the lake. So does Mattie and Paul. Fuck. We jump off. At 30 miles an hour. Roll along for a bit then get up. No-one's hurt. We're all laughing. We watch the bus. It doesn't go in the lake. It goes across the top of the weir to the other side. Just wide enough. Then they all disappear around the other side of the lake. Headlights swooping through the dark. Bollocks. We should have stayed on. Never mind. That jump sure was exciting.

It starts to rain. Me and Douggie have got military trench coats on. We decide to leave the Chevy and walk back to Mattie's. It's four miles. I'll pick it up tomorrow. No problem they say. We'll look after it. The city looks good .Slicked in rain. Neon kinda suits it. We stop by a storm drain. Watching the water swirl around under a streetlight. I can see all the letters of the alphabet swirling around in it.Course i can i'm tripping. I tell Douggie and Neeta. Yeah they say. We can see them too. This stuff's great. We watch for about half an hour. Finally get to Mattie's about 3 am. Soaked but happy. Hardly drank a drop all night. Fell asleep in the dark on the sofa. All cuddled up together. Listening to JJ Cale. 'After Midnight'. Yeah Baby.

Rave on

The acid is starting to bring up memories i had forgotten.They run through my mind like a film. I see it all when i'm awake. I see it all on the back of my eyelids when i sleep. My whole life seems to be being lived all at once. I remember everything from the age of two onwards. I wish i didn't. It's not all good. I sometimes wonder if i'm dreaming. It's a fuckin' nightmare.

Malc's back for the week. He's staying here on the sofa. Wales was going tits up he said. Not surprised. Jesus. How can all this be better, what's wrong with him ? I got the feeling I wasn't even getting half the story. He steals cars. He steals everything. He's leaning over me. He's trying to get me up. I'm tripping. 2 Supermen. I can't speak. I don't understand what he's saying to me. It's like every word stretches. I can't remember how to move my legs. I'm seeing colours. The taxi's waiting. We're going to the pub. He lifts me in a firemans lift. He carries me out to the taxi. It's half past seven at night. The taxi driver laughs. He says i should be like that at the end of the night, not the start. Malc tells him to fuck off. Says i'll be fine, just drive. He's right. We walk in and i come round. Sort of. I can speak and walk slowwwwly. I am floating. People are pleased to see me. Of course they are. I am the man. On Friday nights it's not business. Not really. I can afford to give away 20 trips for every 100 that i sell. And still make a profit. The Cult are playing 'Phoenix' over the sound system - " Well dig this".- I sure am baby.

I go to the bar. Someone pushes in front of me. Knocks me out of the way. It's a big biker. Steve appears. He's not long back from prison. He looks like it. Scars and bleached hair. He's got a new suit. He looks 80's Ssssharp. Shoulder pads and 'Kouros' aftershave. He looks like a Mastiff with a diamond collar. He pulls his jacket off .Throws it on the floor. He's got half a pool cue. It seems to fan out from his arm as he swings it. Trailing. Course it does. I'm tripping. The biker gets a broken nose. He says sorry. He says he was wrong. He says I was first at the bar. He's right. I think he's very lucky he didn't get his blood on Steve's clothes. Steve puts his jacket back on. It's like i am un-fuckin-touchable. I never asked for this. I used to be able to look after myself. Still could if i had to. It's just that....it's just that i seem to be out of my head all the time lately. I know everyone. I order ten bottles of Grolsch. I don't want to come back to the bar. Steve gives me the keys to an XJS . It's parked outside. It's brand fuckin' new. It hasn't even got a number plate. I say i can't drive. I say i'm fucked. He says it doesn't matter. He says don't leave prints. There's driving gloves on the dash. He says if you're caught, just leave it and run. It doesn't matter. He says if you crash it, just set fire to it and run. He says it doesn't matter. It's going to be trashed tomorrow anyway.

I'm sitting at a table with everyone. Mattie, Hann, Douggie, Neeta, Malc, Big Steve. Bottles and pint pots everywhere. It's like our own private club. There are people asking for trips. I've got fifty in my pocket, I can't get them out. I can't remember how. Malc does it for me.He even puts the money in my pocket when they're all sold. He doesn't steal from me. Someone wants 500. Sure. See Steve tomorrow. We'll do it. Our DJ puts on The Art of Noise and Duane Eddy – 'Peter Gunn'. He says it's for me. I wave. He smiles. He's tripping. There are at least 20 people tripping in here that i know. That twangy guitar just seems to bend around the room. Then he says this one's for Jay. It's an American rap band, 'Hawk' singing 'The alarm' – 'Get up Motherfucker, Get out of your bed'. Rap and heavy guitar. Years before Aerosmith and Run DMC. It's great. I'm still sitting at the table with the crew. Staring at my beer. I'm staring for 10 minutes. Everyone talks around me. I can't move my arms. Malc notices. He lifts the bottle up. He puts my fingers around it. He laughs. I laugh. I'm fine now. Aha are singing 'The sun always shines'. Fuckin' tell me about it. The big ceiling fans feel like a gale. They feel warm. I can't breathe. The rush is wearing off. Wow man - what a hit. We leave the pub at midnight. No thought of the state we were in. This was normal for us. No it wasn't. We didn't do normal. We were immortal.

We were untouchable. We were the crew. We knew everyone. Everyone knew us.

The Jag is Gold. It is gleaming. It is ours for the night. It's like Cinder-fuckin-ella. It's going to turn into a pumpkin. It's going to turn into a ball of flame. Mmm. The thought registers. Better be careful. Six up ,110 mph. In the fog. Can't see more than 20 feet. Yello blasting out of the sound system. 'St. Senor the hairy grill'. Manic guitar. That is heavy. It's like driving underwater.This was careful. No it wasn't. We didn't do careful. A pair of red foglights loom up in front of me. It's just before our junction. I cut across them from the fast lane into the exit ramp. We flash past. I look at the driver. He looks at me. It's a moment. It's a police Sierra. Oh fuck. Too late. We're gone up the ramp. He's off into the mist. Still doing sixty as we approach the roundabout at the top. I Forget it's an auto. I stick it into reverse. We're still doing Thirty. Bang. The car Jumps in the air. I know i'm tripping but I swear it did .Two feet off the ground. It lands on the curb of the roundabout. It's rocking. It's still running. I'm wondering if we should call Jaguar to tell them how strong their cars are. I think my thought processes aren't quite right. There we are. We get out. We're standing on the round about. Thinking of torching it. A car pulls up. It's not the Police. It's Steve. He's laughing at the car. He has a friend with a long scar down his face . He's laughing too.They've got Golden Earring playing 'Radar Love' in their car. It drifts across the roundabout. We all push it off the curb. We get back in. It clonks when i put it in drive. The fuckin' thing still goes. It won't tomorrow morning. Steves taking it to the crusher. Him and his friend. Lots of

things end up in that scrapyard. Don't fall asleep in it they say. I don't think they're joking.
Home. We smoke Opium laced black. It's the only time i smoke that stuff. It makes me sleep. I put 'Nancy and Lee' on the stereo. 'Summer Wine' I sleep like the fuckin dead.

Weeks later I move out of the scousers house. I saw something I didn't like. I moved in with Hannah and Matty.

Friday. I'm down the pub. Tripping as usual. I've got faded 501's tucked into my embroidered cowboy boots. Black polo neck. Faded Denim jacket. Studded Punk belt. Bleached hair. The Scouse girl comes up to me. Asks me why I don't move back in .Tells me she misses me. My head is flying. What ?. Says she loves me. I don't know what to say. I'm having trouble thinking. I can't believe what i'm hearing. I thought she didn't like me. Tells me I'm a fookin' twat. Then she kisses me. She does. Wow. It seems to go on for ever. That was some kiss. I felt it in my boots. In front of everyone. How long had I wanted to do that. I'm stood there speechless. The D.J. puts on Charlie Whitehead singing 'I finally found myself something to sing about'. It's one of Steve's Northern Soul 45's. Oh very funny. I stick two fingers up at Steve. He laughs. I wish I wasn't tripping. Oh fuck.

The DJ's playing more Northern Soul. - George Tindley singing 'Pity the poor man'. There's Steve and two of his mates .Fuck can they dance. They're spinning. Doing backflips. Jumping scissor kicks on the beat. Steve always said that Disco was watered down Soul. I can see what he means. This is impressive. Everyone is looking on .I don't know what they're seeing but i'm tripping. Steve's feet are a blur. They're all off to London tomorrow. The 6T's Northern Soul Club are having an all-nighter. On a boat. Dancefloor and everything he says. Blimey. Next day I wake up. I'm not sure if it really happened.

Next week. She's there again. She kissed me. I wish i'd known for sure that she'd be there. If I could think straight I'd do something. But of course i wasn't. I'd lived there for a year. I was crazy about her. But too late. My head was fucked now. I can't help it. I'm tripping all the time. It blocks things out. Like pain. I do nothing about it. I think she took that bad. She was pissed off with me. I was pissed off with myself. It was like I'd started something I couldn't control anymore. It wasn't addiction but...If i stopped i'd have nothing. I'd have to face myself. Just when i'd found a new way to avoid it. Childhood coming back to haunt me. Can't kid yourself when you're tripping. How would i live. How could i live with her. How would we afford it. I couldn't think beyond that. I should've. Oh fuck. What was I doing. I knew at the time I'd always regret it. I was right. I have. I knew what was waiting for me at the end of it all too.... Me.

The following week. Hannah and Mattie have organised a surprise for her boyfriend Pat. Wanna come they ask. I like surprises. Off we go. In Hannah's Cortina estate. It runs out of petrol. We get out to push it down the road to the petrol station. Pat turns to me and says this is fun. You ought to try it tripping i say. You're not are you he says. Laughing. Yeah baby i say. Just for a change then. We get it filled up. Still won't start. Hannah goes up to some guy at the till. He's got jump leads. So would i have. Hannah sure looks nice in her denim miniskirt. Big 80's hair. Mmmm. We're off. The drive seems to go on forever. The giggle mobile. Finally. We're there. Northampton. Pat's got his eyes closed as we go into the theatre. Me too. We sit down in the dark. Suddenly the lights come on. 'The Drifters' walk on stage. All white tuxedo's and smiles. The Fuckin' Drifters! Wow ! I sit mesmerised. 'Under the board walk' 'Saturday night at the movies'. All the hits. I've been listening to them since i was little. This is like a dream. They never stop smiling. The whole gig. Neither do i. I don't know who enjoyed it more. Me or Pat. That was some trip.

Friday. Me. Mattie. Paul the photographer. Go to Douggie & Neeta's for the night. Tripping as soon as we get there. We go for a walk in the woods. The sand on the paths is glowing. We're all giggling. Doing silly walks. We feel warm. Safe. End up in a field. There's piles of haybales everywhere. Harvest time. We jump on them. Falling over. It's like a fairground ride. Starlight seems really bright. We play for hours. End up sitting under some trees in the middle of the field. Laying on our backs looking at the stars. I can't stop laughing. The world just all seems so funny. Later we're walking along the country lane back into the village. There's an old Victorian streetlight. Douggie puts his hand up to point at it. Something flies around his outstretched arm. It's a bat. Blimey ! Look he says. They're playing. We all stick up our hands. Bats come and circle round and round. Wow. Ain't nature great we say. We watch spellbound. They flit and swoop endlessly. Douggie's right .They are playing with us. The bats leave after about half an hour. Seems longer. We walk back to Douggie's house. It looks really tall. We all stop and stare at the roof. It doesn't look that tall in the daytime . Not 'cause we're tripping then, says Douggie. Laughing. Oh Yeah. I forgot. We go in and put on a Marc Bolan video. He's singing a duet of 'Life's a Gas' with Cilla Black. It's beautiful. She's staring into his eyes. Ahh we all say. Fall asleep as it's getting light outside. The birds are singing. They sound beautiful.

Glastonbury Revisited

It's Saturday lunch time. Me, Tony and the chicken farmer. In the pub. The Talking Heads are singing 'Psycho Killer'. Chicken Dexy's are good but there's something else we can do. The farmer has a burger van. It's not big enough to cook for big events. Tony says he wants one for Glastonbury. We have the money. The farmer has a festival licence.The farmer says yes. He says he'll work it with us. We say we'll build it. We're gonna sell all sorts from it. Deal done. Here comes the summer. Yum Yum Yum.

The trailer's ready. It sure looks fine. We know a catering equipment manufacturer. Steve went to school with him. We have the best looking food trailer you ever saw. It's got more turned aluminium than a vintage Bentley. It is the dogs bollocks. The sign has 'Yummy Zoomers' painted over the serving hatches. It's an in joke. You'd understand if you were an acid casualty. Like us.
Glastonbury.

We have a bag full of novocaine and bombers. We're playing Motorhead in the trailer. 'No sleep til Hammersmith'. Not this weekend. We're selling burgers. Hotdogs. Chips. We're selling Novocaine and Trips. No one else on the site is selling Novocaine. Or Trips like ours. Tony made sure of that. With his friends from Amsterdam. They're in charge. For now. He's bought a house there. On the canal. The money pours in. The sweat pours off .I think Simply Red are on the main stage but it's hard to make it out. We don't stop for music. We're not here for fun. Anything that drops on the floor is put on a special shelf . After we've trod and spat on it. If any customers give us shit we serve it to them. As an extra portion. Here you go mate. Have a double on us. To cheer them up. Then they're sorry they were stroppy. They will be by tomorrow when they're queuing for those lovely toilets with the shits. All served with a smile. Ha Ha .Fuckers.

Later on as it calms down Aswad are playing. Me and Emma the disco dolly go for a shower. She's so beautiful. She looks like Nancy Sinatra but prettier. Sixties hair. Big blue eyes. Aqua Marina. Brigitte Bardot. Blondie. Mmmm. Suicide blonde. It's a long story. Not mine to tell. I'd known her since we were little. She came to Glastonbury with me. Wearing a cocktail dress and stillettoes. Very 80's. How did she end up with a drug dealing ex punk rocker? It was at one of my party's. I had always fancied her. The disco dolly and the punk. I think my life's turning into a fairy tale. It's a village thing. It's where we're from. We queue up. I've never been in a communal shower before. Bloody hippies. There's a big Rasta in front of me . We go

in. The showers are communal. Oh fuck. I've never really thought about the size of my cock. Now's the time though. There we all are stripping off. Into the showers before i get the chance to worry about it. Men and women all naked. All feet from each other. The beautiful Emma next to me. I Glance at the guy on the other side. As you do. He's looking at Emma . He's all Tattoos and Biceps. I look down. As you do. He's got a tiny cock. I just about stop myself from laughing. When i look across the Rasta's seen me checking. He's chuckling. He gives me the thumbs up. He turns back to his shower head. I scrub away with carefree abandon after that. Whatever it's better than the communal toilets. All that dodgy food......
We manage one walk around the site all weekend. We are so busy it's disgusting. The food isn't though. The meat's from the village. We sell good quality stuff. Like our drugs. The Psychedelic Furs are singing 'India' on our built in sound system.
It goes so well , it's decided we'll have an ice cream van too next year. 'Uncle Yummer's Ices'. I don't know if it's still funny. It's like the child catcher from Chitty Bang Bang. Seems a bit sinister to me. Selling drugs from an ice cream van. Childhood's End. We don't do kidnap and cages though. Not yet. Not in England. Fuck's sake. We made over 50,000 quid that weekend. Steve was burying himself in it in his front room. We were all laughing like we couldn't believe it. We couldn't. That was an awful lot of money then. You could buy a house. Steve did. Tony had opened a bank account in Luxembourg. We fed that fucker.

So one month later. Round at Steve's. We're listening to James Brown 'Get on the good foot'. Steve's talking to someone he knows. On the phone. He wants to take the trailer to Silverstone. He wants to sell Coke to the rich people. He wants more. Bloody Hell. Him and his cars. Mind you i'm as bad..This isn't a game. He's not scared of Prison. Comes with the job he says. Fuck'em he says. Let's do it. He wants to buy a house in Spain. And some hotels. His friends from London are already out there. It's where the money is he says. And the sun. It's like Miami Vice. Except the coppers are all bent. You can buy whatever you want down there. Steve wants a Corvette. And a pool. He wants the wild west. Just like me. I always thought i'd be the good guy though. I'd never thought about Coke really. There was no master plan. Shit happens.

Ghost in The Machine

Me and Emma go down to her dad's place for the weekend. To get away. He lives in a village near Torquay. He's entering his powerboat in the Cowes - Torquay race. We drive down . He has some house. 4 car garage. There's a Ferrari 308. A Jensen SP111. An E type. There's a fuckin' helicopter on the lawn. Wow. We swim in his pool before eating supper on the terrace. He looks like Frankie Vaughan. Emma says he builds houses. Amongst other things. I don't ask. We go into town for Lunch the next day. He owns the local pub too I notice people seem to have a lot of respect for this man. It almost seems like fear. If you know what i mean. I don't ask questions. We get on like a house on fire. He's great. We spend the rest of the day out on his Yacht. Watching him in the race. His powerboat makes it to Cowes. Breaks down halfway back. He says it doesn't matter. He says it's just fun to be here. He'd grown up dreaming of being rich. Fuck .I like this man. I think he likes me too. The next day he takes us for a ride in the powerboat. Fuelling problem he said. Fuck's sake. This thing is fast. Keep your knees bent he says. Otherwise you might break your neck. He's not kidding. I can't see the speedo. I'm hanging on for dear life. It takes off over a wave. When it lands it feels like we've hit a rock. All of a sudden he's wheeleying it . It's a fuckin boat ! Jesus ! What a buzz. Sure is he says. Laughing. Move down here with Emma he says. I'll set you up with a house and a job. It'd be great to have my little girl down here. What do you want to do he says. Emma says no. She still lives with her mother in our village. His ex wife. Shame. That was fun . I'm starting to think i've had enough of my lifestyle. I'm starting to think that i might want a normal one. I wonder if there's enough of me left to sort out. Hmmm....

I'm starting to hear rumours. About Emma. I choose to ignore them. She wouldn't. Would she ? I remember her from when we were little. We never went to the same school. I danced with her at a village disco when i was 14. Everyone laughed. She was only 11. I told them to fuck off. She'd be beautiful one day i said. She sure was now. I had loved her from afar. I guess i didn't really know her after all. I might have noticed if i'd been straight. Big Steve told me she was messing about. I didn't want to hear it . I wanted it to be right. Right ? What was i thinking. I was drugged up most of the time. She drank me under the table every night. Pints of Red Stripe. All five beautiful foot of her. I don't know where she put it. She was with me most nights. Like peas in a pod. Except for her girl's nights out. But she stayed at her girlfriend's house. Didn't she ? No she didn't . Finally i found out. Oh Fuck. Gone wrong again. I guess i couldn't blame her. If i was honest. It hurt to be honest. That's why i tried to avoid it. Two wrongs don't make a right. I was definitely going wrong. So was Emma. And I wasn't helping her. I don't think anyone could. Plenty tried it seemed. Often. I think my Fairy Tale is becoming one of the Brother's Grimm. I probably deserve it. I'm starting to wonder if there are any happy endings. Probably not for a drug dealer eh ? Maybe i should write my own. But that would mean stopping. Everything. Wouldn't it. Then what would i have ? This is all i've got. I know it's all wrong. But it's a world that we've made for ourselves. Out of nothing. And i love these guys. I don't want to be alone again. There's a Gene Vincent song 'Hurtin for you Baby'. Just about sums it up. Check out the second verse.

One week later. Round at Tony's. The Cramps LP 'Smell of Female' is on. Faster Pussycat. Yeah baby. It's great. The farmer rings up. Problem. The trailers gone. Oh - Oh ! You would have seen a switch go in Steve's head if you'd been there. It was like that. F words. His fist goes through the kitchen door. Blood and glass shards everywhere. Right ! he screamed . I'm gonna find that fucker. I believe him. Tony is sitting with his hard stare on. Chairman Tone. It is indeed a hard stare. He doesn't like it when people mess up his arrangements. I don't know which one is more scary. Oh goody.... This should be fun.....

Actually it wasn't. Steve found out where it was. Gypsies. So...I remember it in little flashes – Six of us. Black bombers and no beer. Clear heads. The land rover smelling of diesel. Things clunking in the back as we went over bumps along a track.

Pickaxe handles and swords. Fuck me, this wasn't playing. Dark. Setting fire to our own trailer. In front of the people who nicked it. Fuck it said Steve. It's insured. You wanted it, you have it he said to them. That was the first time I saw Steve pull a gun. He shot one of them in the legs. One of them started to pull out a sawn off next to me. Looking at Tony with murder in his eyes. I did him with a pickaxe handle before he could point it. Just about took his head off. There was a lot of people screaming. We set fire to their Barn. I didn't say a single word. Quiet one me. What do you say anyway ? Until we got back to Steve's. Then I said I didn't think it was a good idea to start a war with Gypsies. He said he didn't think it was a good idea for them to start one with us. OK. About right I suppose. Whatever. Fun is not a word I would use.

Drift Away

OK I need a rest from all the madness of the new city. It's getting to me. I'm a village boy at heart. I'm walking in the woods. With Douggie . A thought comes to me. The pathways are sand. Like a beach. The trees are pines. Mmmm. You could have a pretend beach party here. Wouldn't that be funny. I've sold the Chevy and bought a Beach Buggy. White with rainbow stripes. Big wheels. I speak to Douggie. He's into it. We plan it for the weekend. Just me and him and his wife, Neeta. She's Indian. She's very beautiful.

We go down there saturday morning and collect logs for a fire. I spend all week making cassettes of music that we love. T Rex. Velvet Underground. The Doors. Nancy Sinatra & Lee Hazelwood. We're ready.

Douggies house. 8 o'clock. Matty's here too. He's cool. He's my landlord. Him and Hannah. He brings a load of Red Stripe. Douggie & Neeta bring Rolls. Potatoes in tin foil. Hand painted jam jars with candles in. To hang from the trees. I bring

Acid. Supermen. We eat it and then set off to the woods. We get the fire lit before the trip starts working. It's getting dark. The fire is big. We sit around it. It looks like forever in the flames.The Velvet Underground are singing 'Candy Says'. They're singing 'Stephanie says'. They're singing 'Lisa says'. One after the other. The music is soooo mellow. It sounds too slow. It sounds greaat. It's my tape.

Fuck this stuff's strrrrrong. My stomachs churning. I think. I can't be sure. I see and hear everything all at the same time. Time and place have disappeared. So have i. Douggies crying. Neeta tells him she loves him. I tell him i love him. Douggie says it's too strong. He's right. It is. I tell him it'll be alright. I take him to the steep grass bank next to us. Look at the stars Douggie i say. It's all i can think of. He lies down and looks up. He's silent. For what seems like forever. He's smiling. See ? i say. Yeah he says. We all lie down there looking up at the stars. The Doors are playing. 'Crystal Ship'. Yeah baby. The music seems to swirl up into the night sky with the flames and sparks from the fire. It's the night of the shooting stars. We didn't know. It's like a firework show. There seem to be hundreds of meteors up there. There are little clouds scudding across the stars .They look Pink.They look orange. They make patterns. The Crescent moon is hanging contentedly. It looks like a stage prop. It is a stage prop. We can see the wire. It's an American fifties moon from a stage show. With a big smiling face. Course it is. We're tripping. 'Strange Days' drifts up into the night. Too right. Suddenly there's a moment. We're all smiling. We see the meaning of life. All of it. All at once. We all have the same thought. We're all crying. We're so happy.

A couple of hours later. It seems years. It's still dark. The trip's not so intense now. The candles are glowing in their jars. The colours are beautiful .It looks like a fairies party in the woods. I can see sparks in the other's eyes. We're dancing to T.Rex. Around the fire. 'Get it on'. I'm flailing my arms slowly like a windmill. We see ten arms fanned out. Trailing. Like the special effects on old Top of the Pops. Wow. We all have a go. We love Marc Bolan. We're sad that he's gone. The music seems to be coming from all around us. Marc sings 'Life's a Gas' . It is.
Neeta climbs a little silver birch tree. It's only 4ft high. I give her a hand up. The tree bends over like a bow. She balances . She's got ripped jeans on with fishnets underneath. There's a rip across the back pockets. A bit of fishnet covered Neeta is hanging out. She has the most gorgeous arse i've ever seen. It's about six inches from my face. I love her. She laughs. I laugh. Douggie laughs. Look Douggie i say. I think you'd better do this .I just can't.....i double up with laughter. We drink Red Stripe . We smoke JPS cigarrettes. We eat the potatoes from the fire. They feel like marshmallows. They taste grrrreat. We laugh.

Douggie has some torches. Bits of stick with cloth round the end. We light them. We go to the edge of the grass bank. We stick them in the ground. We climb up the bank to the top. It seems a long way. When we look down at the fire it looks hundreds of feet below us. It's like looking down into a crater. The fire looks like a tiny sparkling distant jewel. We love that fire. Look says douggie. There's more torches. We look. We see hundreds of flaming torches amongst the trees. Fuck. Who's that . Is it villagers come to get us? Have we gone back to the middle ages? No says douggie. He's laughing. There's only two really. He's right . We're seeing things. Course we are. We're tripping. We laugh. There's only two little flames down there now. Oh goody. My head feels like that old gale is blowing through it.

We go for a walk through the woods to the edge. We leave the stereo playing. The sand on the paths is fuckin' glowing .It feels so soft underfoot. I can feel it through my cowboy boots. It's beautiful. It's guiding us. Making sure we don't get lost. We sit at the edge of the woods. You can see the lights of Milton Keynes from here. We don't like it anymore. It looks false. It is. Arthur Lee and Love - 'Sitting on a hillside'. People have been spending money in the pubs and clubs down there. They will be feeling rough by now. We're not. We feel superior. Course we do. We're tripping. We know the meaning of life. We love it. Our lives are the same as the trees. Like the stars. We're all the same. We feel like we've come home. We go back to the fire. It looks so cosy. It's welcoming us. The Doors have finished. We put on Nancy & Lee. They're singing 'Some Velvet Morning'. That orchestral backing. Their voices. Ethereal. It sounds achingly beautiful.

It starts to get light. 'Summer Wine' floats out of the stereo. The music ends. The birds are singing. The first rays of the sun are filtering through the treetops. It is beautiful. We love this world. We love the woods.We love life. It is the greatest gift. It feels like i've lived a whole lifetime in one night. We haven't even smoked one pack of JPS. We've only drunk six cans of Red Stripe. We feel good. We don't want to go back to the real world. We tidy the fire away. We'll be back. Too right. Wouldn't it be great if everyone could come to a party in the woods......

Well, like most things it was to start with. We had a few more little gatherings down there. Word spread but winter arrived all too soon. Mum and Dad were going away. Said it was ok to have a party at their house. It was a big place. Up on top of the hill. Surrounded by trees. Nice and secluded. I warned the neighbours anyway. I invited everyone I knew. So did my sisters. You expect about half of them to turn up. They all did. There were about 200 people. DJ Picci and Gordon bought some of the Camden Palace sound system. Set up in the dining room. Stilletto marks in the parquet from Neeta dancing all night in front of the speakers. There were people skinning up on the kitchen table all night. Bags of weed the size of rucksacks. The Scouser had the bathroom mirror down on the table. Mountains of speed. Everyone was there. Friday and Saturday night. The village pub sold out of takeaways. Not a glass was broken. What a party. We said we'd do it down the woods in the summer. Everyone said they'd come. The neighbours said they never heard a thing. It was like living in an enchanted fairytale.

May. It's sunny. It's party time. Everyone turns up. Hundreds. We Meet in the village pub. They're in both bars. The beer garden. On the verge opposite . Outside Ivan's house. The pub is drunk dry. The landlady asks if I'm having a little party. Says to tell her next time. She'll order extra drink. We all go off down the woods. Little candles in jars to light the way. Everyone's here. There's all the trendies. Soul boys. Bikers. Goths. Punks. Hippies. Stillettoes in the sand. Fishnets and Farah's mixed in the firelight. At least 100 of them are tripping. So am i. Everyone's having a good time. I've made these tapes. Got Motorhead followed by the Bare Neccessities. Followed by Divine. The Doors. Donna Summer. Thunderbirds theme. Makes people giggle. Dancing in the firelight as the sparks drifted up to the stars.

We had a few more like that that year. Just before the raves started. They were great. They just kept on getting bigger. My memories of them are acid dazed. I think I had done too much. They ended with us moving base to Woburn picnic area. Getting too big for the village. Hardly knew anyone anymore. People were sawing down trees for firewood. Someone got shot. What a sad end. Who takes a gun to a party. Not the sort of person I wanted to mix with, that's for sure. Still, I don't think they ever found love and peace in 1967. We sure didn't find it in 1986. Shame.

Playboys

It's Friday. Business done. Douggie calls round. We're going to the Camden Palace. Our DJ Friend and Evil Eddie Richards are doing the sounds. We cruise down the M1 in Douggie's Lotus. I love this car. We're tripping. Only half. Don't want to overdo it. In London. The Palace is great. The sounds are brilliant. Vision are singing 'Lucifer's Friend.' We're dancing the night away. It's great. We get some coke. It's cleaaaannn. My face is numb. So is Douggie's. He says there's something i've got to see. Outside into the lotus. We're going to The Hippodrome.

It's just before midnight and we're in. No problem. The sounds are louder. It's really going some in here. Suddenly it's midnight. It goes quiet. Watch this says Douggie.... The March of the Valkyries comes blasting out. Wagner. This is some build up. It goes dark. Suddenly a flying saucer appears above us. In the club. Fuck me. It's spinning. It's enormous. Oh Fuckin' ell. It's only the lights. It descends. Flashing and spinning above us. Suspended from the ceiling. That is definitely something you should see tripping. Fuckin amazing. 'Close Encounters' eat your heart out. We're laughing. There's a group of girls next to us. They're laughing. They've got big eyes. They've got cut glass English accents. They're posh .They're Ballet dancers they say. They're tripping too. We talk. We get on great. They're having a party tomorrow they say. In Hampstead. Be there at eight they say. We'll have a lot of fun.

So. Saturday. Ripped Jeans. Espadrilles. Baggy Tee shirts. Earrings. Eye liner. My hair's bleached white. Douggies is Jet Black. We're off. Down the M1 in my Beach Buggy. The girls open the door. This is a big house. It's got wrought iron balconies. Hampstead is nice. They laugh at the car. It's great they say. It's Hilarious. We laugh too. It is. We go in. We're not out of place. The parties full. Simply Red are playing 'Money's too tight to mention.' - Not here it isn't. This is way cool. There's Champagne. There's Cocaine. We're talking to everyone. The atmosphere is great. The atmosphere is verrrry friendly. The atmosphere is too rich too care. We get chatted up by some rich gay guys. We smile and say no thanks. No problem they say. It is very friendly here. Suddenly It's three in the morning. The party's thinning out. The girls have got their arms round our waists. Will you stay they say. They're laughing. Yes please we say. We're laughing. They've got their hair pulled back. They're wearing diamonds. And stillettos. Eighties cocktail dresses. They are beautiful. And fun. They have a gleam in their eyes. Everyone has. It's the coke.

We're all giggling as we go up the sweeping staircase. There's four of them. There's two of us. We're out numbered. Oh-Oh ! The bedroom is bigger than my flat. I have not seen a bigger bed. Ever. It's round . Honestly. We're there. We're all ripping each others clothes off. Literally. We're all giggling. You know when kissing is just like wowwww. It's like that. Terence Trent D'arby is playing somewhere. Coming from hidden speakers. They are indeed ballet dancers. They are supple like you've never seen. They're supple like we've never seen. They are very naughty indeed. So are we. We fall asleep. It's light already.

We all have breakfast on the balcony. We're sitting on each others laps. They're going to do a tour with the Royal Ballet they say. It's been great they say. Yep. It sure has we say. They wave to us from the door. They lift their nighties and flash us. We drive off laughing. Now that's a weekend.

When the Music's Over

Finally i have a bad trip. Pretty good considering. It's been every weekend for 3 years. Like people say – a good one is the best thing in the world. A bad one is the worst. Too fuckin' right. Jesus. I thought i'd gone mad. Memories of Pigsy at Glastonbury. Of being chased in the woods by some older boys with guns when I was little. Getting shot at. A couple of lifetimes ago. I guess I finally caught up with myself. That's enough for me. Primal fear. 12 hours of it. I ended up sitting under a tree on my own. Waiting for the dawn. When i finally managed to think straight enough to remember what dawn was. I knew it should wear off around then. It did. I thought of everyone else. Tucked up in bed safe and warm. Cuddling someone who loves them. In their own house. What the fuck have i been doing ? Three years or more. Even the speed and coke just makes me feel dirty these days. Christ. Is that all i can do. Escape ? Bollocks . I can do better than that. I've watched everyone else sort themselves out. Now it's my turn. But i don't want it tainted by all this. I feel like someone's telling me to stop.

About bleedin' time says Tony when i tell him. Never get high on your own supply. He can talk. He's importing E's now. Been selling them to all the Ravers. That's ALL the ravers. He's making thousands. I'm not interested in E's. Not strong enough for my liking. Like that Bobby Vee song – 'Halfway to Paradise'. I'm not interested . I've just got real tired. It doesn't seem like fun any more. I started taking stuff to escape. Now i feel it's taking me. Stealing my life. Present and future. No more drugs for me. No more of this lifestyle. Let's see how i can do. Yeah Baby. I sell my cars. Both of them. Like it's symbolic or something. I buy a Toyota Celica. Nice.

Backtrack

What it is. What it's always been. I left Reading in late 1964. With a new name and a new identity. I wasn't a criminal. I was six months old. The Beatles were conquering America. Maria Callas was doing her last comeback concert at the Covent Garden Opera house. Marlene Dietrich was wowing them at Olympia in London, Jacques Brel at the Olympia, Paris and Sam Cooke was slaying them at the Copa.

I was the little boy who's mummy and daddy didn't want him. Gave me away. I'm adopted. Some people are ok with that. I wasn't. I was fucked up by it. How honest shall I be in what I say ? I was born Oothur Willon Brown. My real father was called Arthur. My real mother Jeannette. She would be harder than all the rest to write about. So I won't. Let's just say it didn't work out. For either of us. I spent the first six weeks of my life in a cot in a converted loft. There were six other cots. All with unwanted babies in. Fostering was different then. We were fed and cleaned. But never picked up or given any attention. Just laid there looking up out of the skylight. When my adoptive parents came to see me, they were told I was either profoundly deaf or Autistic. Or both. For some reason they took me anyway. Appointments at Gt. Ormond St Hospital. I still have my card. Finally I had the good fortune to see an Indian doctor. He told them. Nothing wrong with me. Emotional shutdown. It's what babies do if they're left alone. Survival instinct. Just needed someone to notice me. They did. I owe them my life.

I need to find out why. Who do I look like. Have they loved me somewhere out there. Have they thought about me. Or not. How can I think about that when I have my adopted mum and dad. Does that make me bad ? Ungrateful ? It's not like that. I tell them. They understand. It was them who told me about the loft. I sometimes have dreams of looking up at the clouds or the stars through a little skylight. There were bars around me. I knew what they were now. I still love laying on my back and staring at the sky. Even now. I feel like nothing can touch me. And nothing really matters. Drift away with the clouds. Shutdown.

My mum gives me a motheaten little green top and shawl. Says it's what I came in when they adopted me. Bloody 'ell. I can't put it off much longer. What if I do and it's too late. I'll have missed the chance to meet them. Hmmm.

New Leaf

I met a girl. She worked as a P.A. at my dad's company. Everyone fancied her. She was beautiful. She sort of reminded me of the Scouse girl. But she was normal. She wore nice clothes. She was so sexy. What a doll. Everyone said no chance. They were wrong. I wanted her. I wanted a normal life. I chose happiness. I chose hard work. I asked her out. She said yes. I was so in love. I made her laugh. She thought that would be enough. We went out for two years. My attempts at straight work didn't do too well. It was all new to me. I did all sorts. Factory work through a temping agency. Porter in a piano factory. All sorts. I met some good people though. Eventually we finished. I still loved her. She lived with an old boyfriend. I lived with an old girlfriend. It wasn't right though. Wasn't fair on them either.

I bought a Ford Capri. 3.O S. Just resprayed. Metallic blue. Fishnet Recaro's. 2.8i suspension. It was a babe. I decided to go to France. Cruise around. Visit Francis. I do. Stop off at Ile de Res. Chartres. Brive. Down to Gers. All over. Stop at some of my Mum & Dad's friends for new years eve. They've got a little Chateau. Wow. So. 2 weeks. The car ran like a dream. Cruising all day at 70. I get back up as far as Rennes. Stopped at a red light. Crossroads. I watch a lady in a little Citroen coming towards me. She's gonna stop. She's not stopping. She isn't even looking up. Fuck. Smashes right into the front of me. Bang. Oh bollocks. I get out. There's a big Vee in the front of the car. The bonnet is all buckled in. She gets out. She's got a map in her hand. That's why she wasn't looking up. She tells me she's not from here. She's from Provence. She tells me she's on holiday. You're on fuckin' holiday I say. At least you're in the right country... What can you do. We fill out the European accident forms. I tie the bonnet down with my tow rope. The car don't look such a babe now. I drive back home slowly. Ish. Finally. Back in England. On the M25. This little Nova passes me. There's someone waving. It's Rita. Blimey. Haven't seen her since M.K. Only four years ago. Bloody hell. Seems like longer.

Me and the girl from my dads company. We got back together two years later. I was so happy. I'd got a proper job in the travel industry. Sounds good doesn't it. I joined the Railway. As a freight guard. Started at the bottom.There is nothing romantic about walking around a freight yard in the rain at 2 in the morning. I had never worked so hard in my life. I met a lot of good real people. They helped me through it. All those rule books to learn. Random drink and drug tests. I don't think it's so hard these days. It was then. Trust me. It was a life apart. Away from everything and everyone. It would not be an overstatement to say that it has been both the making and the saving of me. Got me on the straight and narrow, workwise, and I have never got off.

We got married. I was so proud. We lived in her flat. I was cycling 8 miles a day to work and back. Boxing twice a week again. I was fit. Things were so fuckin' great. Tony said take time off from business. I hoped for good.

Steve bought a Range Rover Vogue. Brand new. Very nice. At least i think he bought it. But he had two. And a new bike. I didn't ask. He'd been doing real well selling Coke to the rich. Silverstone. Polo matches. Anywhere there was money. He was like a bloodhound.

Tony moved to Spain. He had to. He'd been busted. He called me from the police station. Said to go and clean the house. I went. I took everything. There were three bags of gear. One bag full of fivers. The house was clean when the police arrived. The last favour from our 'friend'. The head of the squad had retired. Moved to Spain. Running a little hotel up near Ronda. Tony said stay incognito. He said stay straight. Work hard. Oh and burn the gear. What about the money i said. What money he said. Chuckling. So. Tony went. I put some of the money in a savings account. Then we bought a bigger house. In Leighton. Near her family. And mine. Normal life .At last.

I went to see the Sex Pistols 20 years reunion concert at Finsbury Park. With Iggy Pop and the Buzzcocks. What a legend. All of them. I gather the Pistols didn't used to be so good. They sure are now. Blimey.

Storm Brewing

Right. Now's the time. I get in touch with the Adoption agency. They have a letter for me. It's from my father. Addressed to me. Fuckin' ell. It gives a short message and says he's moving to America. This was 10 years ago. He left his Uncle's address for me. I have Uncles I have never known. We share the same blood. Blimey. I contact him . Tell him I am an old friend of my father's from the sixties. He pauses. Then he says 'I know who you are. You're his son aren't you. I knew you'd ring one day.'

Bloody hell. I'm trying to talk but there's a big lump in my throat. 'You can ring me back when you can talk if you like' he says. 'Don't worry, I'll be here' He says. 'What's your name ?' He asks. I tell him. I don't know if I'll be able to do this again. I swallow hard. Take a deep breath. 'Can you tell me about my father ?' I ask. 'Well, he was studying Philosophy at University when you were born. Gave it all up to be a rock and roll singer though' he said. Fuck me. I know music history. Especially the 60's. I put 2 & 2 together. It makes four. Click. I know who he's talking about. Those names on my adoption certificate. It's Crazy Arthur Brown. The God of Hellfire. Bloody 'ell. Bloody 'ell. I've got his LP. Is that why I love 60's music ? Is that why I'm the way I am ? Blimey.

I get to meet him. At his brother's house. My Uncle Colin. I cried . He cried. It is very hard to try and put down on paper how that felt and what was said. Found out I had old French blue blood in my veins too.
I went with him to visit his mother. My grandmother. Blimey. I took that little green top and shawl. I showed them to her. I made those she said. Recognised her own knitting 30 years later. Oooh how we cried. She said she'd thought of me every birthday. Prayed for me. Fuck. I was speechless. What can you say to that ? Those 30 years will always be there. I was made by all that. Can't erase them. I can forgive though. Life's too short. Everything I've ever done seems to have led to this point. I wish I'd known that there had been one all along.

We had two lovely children. Girls. They were so beautiful and perfect. And innocent. I never felt i deserved them. I think it showed. I didn't seem to make her laugh much anymore. I was working shifts and weekends. I had no time for boxing. I had no time for anything much. She started to love me less. I couldn't blame her. I didn't know how to make it right. She didn't either. When i tried she just said if you don't like it why don't you leave. Ouch. What was i supposed to do. This was the best i could manage for now . It would get better with time. I thought we were doing ok. I helped feed the kids. I changed nappies. I never went out to the pub. I let her spend my money on clothes. I got us a new car. But i was years behind in the getting on stakes. All her friends had bigger houses. Better cars. They'd all been working hard for years. Whilst I'd been partying. She wanted it all now. Maybe i should've stayed drug dealing. I'd be rich now. Maybe you should've she said. Ouch. I started listening to my Janis Joplin LP's a lot. Blue. I started to go running through the woods. Miles.I needed to see something that wasn't wrong. Why am i dreaming of escape. This was what i wanted. I thought it was what she wanted too.

Fuck. A phone call from Tony. Out of the blue. It's been a while. There were some things that needed sorting out. Quietly. Did I want to help ? I wasn't gonna say no. Tony was in charge of Glastonbury now. Amongst other events. Uncle Yummers was now just selling food. Very profitably. Tony got a cut from that as well as everything else sold there. I made a three day visit to the Costa. Via

Bordeaux. Train and plane. Trace that. I popped in to see Francis. We said it was for work. I suppose it was really. Sort of. Looking after my investment. Couldn't trust anyone else to do it. Then they'd know. Francis knew. I had an English passport. I had a French passport. I used both. I wasn't me. I wasn't a smuggler. I was something else. I was something worse. I spoke to people. I persuaded people. I put an end to people. I can do it without losing my temper. Slowburn. Emotional shutdown. The quiet one. No pangs of guilt afterwards. Nobody knew me down there.

Big Steve got five years for robbery. He was caught putting the last of 14 BMW's onto a transporter. It was 0330 am. The cars weren't his. He hadn't even broken a window at the dealership. Seems a shame. Him and his cars. I went to the court. He just looked bored. When his sentence was handed out he just shrugged. He waved at me and smiled. 'See you later son' he shouted. He didn't mind prison. Lots of his friends were there. I was sorry he was going. I felt like the coppers were looking at me. Paranoid? I don't think so. Keeps me sharp. I keep working hard. Mr. Straight.
My C.V. Becomes a work of art. 6 years of hard work in the industry spoke louder than all previous entries. Just as well. Most of them were fake. I got a better job. In London. International travel. Ho Ho Ho. Almost twice the money. This'll make it better i thought. Didn't think about the 3 hours commuting every day. I'd have done anything to make it all right.

My marriage was still going wrong. Work was eating into my life. She said i wasn't enough anymore. She was right. I was working my tits off. I led a double life really. Playing the waiting game. She didn't know. I couldn't tell her. She knew Tony. She didn't know the connection. How could i explain. One day we'll be rich. It's tied up in an account in Luxembourg. She didn't do patience. I don't think she believed in me any more. I don't know if I did. We'd been together 10 years on and off. I didn't know what to do. I still loved her just as much. She was still as beautiful. I got promotion at work. It seemed to be the only thing i could get right. Maybe i'd been trying too hard. It had all been for her though. I was listening to a lot of old Cuban music. Mambo, Son, Tango, Caliente. Gangster music from another time. Was it any better then? i try to convince myself maybe it was. I think i was trying to get lost in it. Escape.

Arthur got me VIP tickets for the who at Wembley. She didn't want to go. I went with my brother and his mates. At the backstage party afterwards I bumped into John Entwistle. The rest of the band were upstairs somewhere in the depths of Wembley. I asked him if he thought Arthur was any good in the sixties. He gave me a surprised look and said ' Yes of course he was. Very fucking good.' That's good enough for me. Wish I'd met the rest of the band though.

Tony said you're working too hard . Have a holiday. He said let's start to spend it. It's time. He knew something i didn't. He was ill.

O.K. I took some money from the savings account. We went to Kefalonia. Just us .Me and her. No kids. Our first holiday since they were born. She never even asked where the money came from. It was a beautiful island. We went on boat trips. We ate out. Every night. I tried to talk to her. If you don't like it why don't you leave she said. For the hundredth time. We came home to the rain. She told me she didn't love me any more. She said i was just maybe as good as it gets. I said no. Everything i had done i'd done for her. Didn't she know that ? All my hard work? I'd still be a drifter otherwise. She said i had done it for myself. Christ. Was she right ? No. I'd done it for us. But I'd tried to be someone I wasn't. She'd tried too Talk about throwing it in my face. I think my head went. I said goodbye. I don't know how. I was in a daze. I was hurt. I didn't want to stay and for the girls to see their Mummy and Daddy tear each other apart. When i left i took my clothes. My music. And four guns from the loft. She got the house and the car. I got the savings.

She got someone else. Two months after i moved out. One of my kids told me on the phone. That hurt. Fuck. My head went big time. I got signed off from work. Had a bit of a breakdown in the Doctor's Surgery. He prescribed anti–depressants . And Counselling. Ok. Whatever.

The Who's song from Tommy keeps going round in my head.'Can you see the real me, Doctor, Doctor ?'. Fucked if I can. The phrase 'Life imitating art' springs to mind. Mine sure ain't been no performance of 'The Magic Flute'
I don't know what to do. I've got to try and keep it together. For my Girls. I listen to Elvis a lot. There's a reason for that ;

When I was little. I felt lonely. Didn't fit. Course I didn't. I was adopted. My mum and dad only played serious classical music. Laying in front of the open fire in the evenings. Rachmaninoff's 'Vespers' playing. Drift away. Dreaming of Russian snowscapes in starlight. Escape into the firelit shadows. Dr. Zhivago. But. Our housekeeper. My Nanny. Bought a new record every week. Pop music. Wow ! This was fun music. Her son practiced all his dance moves Friday evenings. In their front room. I'd go down there for tea. Piss him off. My uncle Malc. Trying to copy his dancing. I wanted to live down there. It may not have been perfect. It was a real family though. The grass looked greener. One summer's evening. Her husband took me up the field at the back of the house. That was the first time I ever shot a twelve bore. Knocked me over .Shoulder black and blue. I didn't tell my mum and dad. Excellent.

But. I heard Elvis too. That voice. Those songs. Struck a chord in me. At home. I got this cardboard box. Painted the inside with red hearts. Cut out for my neck. I'd lay on the floor under the bed. Put the box on my head. Sing Elvis songs to myself. Dream about love and loss. Elvis style. False fifties memories. Love the way I wanted it to be. Not like this real world. Emotional shutdown. Always made me feel better then. Still does. I play Elvis a lot. Just don't have the box anymore. I am crazy I think. But I'm used to it. Think about it. Like I have. Someone I never knew. Left behind a legacy of music and words that speak to me. As they do to millions worldwide. The longer he's been gone , the more he's eulogised. But loved. Sounds like someone else ? We can all choose who we pray to. I choose Elvis. More relevant to these times. Whatever it takes to get by really. You don't have to believe it's real. Just something to believe in. Choose your illusion....Child of the 60's me.

I start seeing a French girl that i've known for a year or two. It was never anything like that. I didn't do affairs. But i didn't do lonely very well either. We got divorced. 7 years plus. I'd known her for 12 . I loved my two children. I still loved her. It hurt. A lot. I missed them all so much. It was torture picking the children up once a week. I couldn't get my head around it . Didn't seem to make any sense. I said a few things to a few friends that I should not have done. They have since forgiven me. I haven't forgiven myself. I moved in with my sister.

My head went. I'd got time off work. Sick. Too fuckin' right I am. I went to stay at Tony's hotel in Andalucia. He had been busy over the years. He was the organiser. I was the quiet one. On hold. That was useful. Me and Tony went horse riding in the mountains. We went to the best restaurants. We drank the best wine. We saw Paco Pena play a Flamenco show in a backstreet bar in Ronda. That was excellent. Seemed a long way from UK Decay gigs. It was. We hired a Rolls Royce convertible from Marbella Cars. Wafting along the road between Ronda and El Burgo. Just mountains and olive trees as far as you could see. Wow. Had the top floor of a hotel in the old town. Posh. Private lift. Roof terrace. Three balconies. Views across the mountains. Big Steve and co. came up for a meeting. Money talk, as ever. We spent it like water. It was great. I wish i could've taken some home. It wasn't that sort of money. Tony said he missed the rain. I said i missed my life. How could it all have been a mistake. My two lovely children came out of it all. The break did me good.

Tony had four different passports. He was English .He was Spanish. He was Dutch. He was German. He wasn't Tony. He had a house and a hotel in Andalucia. He had a House in Amsterdam. He had a five bedroom Villa in Goa. We had money piling up in Luxembourg. I'm not sure if that was the point. I didn't know what was anymore. Nor did Tony. Vive le Punk ? Hmmm. I think to myself. What would Elvis do ? I went home. Such as it was. At least i had my job.

Oh fuck. Phone call from my mum. My nanny's husband has died. I don't know what to think. So many memories of him. More like a Grandad. He told me my first dirty joke. Made my first go kart. I made a speech at his funeral. Don't know how I got the words out.

Vive Ta Vie

Serious rebound. My French girlfriend. Who wouldn't ? She was beautiful. She was a dancer. And a singer. In the theatre. She'd got divorced. Her ex- husband was a coke dealer in London. It never occurred to me that he might not be the bad one. Her family lived in Marseille. They owned the casino. They owned nightclubs.They owned bars. They owned an island . They owned high speed boats. They wore gold rings on their little fingers. They had machine guns in their houses. They knew Tony. We got a flat in Kensington. Funny noises from the neighbours.She did shows in London. She did shows in Paris. We went all over. She was great. At work I got a fortnight off every eight weeks. We went on lots of holidays. We did the Conde Nast guide. Hotels & restaurants.

One evening I get back to the flat. I walk into the shared hallway. There's our neighbours. Two gay guys. Giovanni and Eric. Both naked. Almost. Giovanni is on all fours. Wearing a pair of Donkey's ears and a tail. Making donkey noises. Eric is chasing him down the hall singing opera. Wagner. They freeze. Oooh sorry, they say. I smile. Don't let me spoil your fun I say. They go into their flat and shut the door. I go into mine, That explains the strange noises then. I put on my Amanda Lear Lp. She's singing 'Give a bit of Mmm To Me'. 70's Camp Disco at it's best. I turn it up. Thought they'd appreciate it. I could still hear Eric singing his opera at the top of his voice and Giovanni Braying. Muffled though. I see Londoners haven't changed then.

Couple of nights later. Me and my girlfriend are sitting out on our terrace. We're drinking Mojito's. Cut the mint from the garden. Giovanni and Eric come down the steps. They apologise again. I laugh. No problem I say, fancy a drink ? We all sat out drinking and smoking until the sun came up. Got hammered .

We went to Strasbourg for a long weekend. Rented an apartment. All beamed houses and little canals. Lovely. We took a boat trip to look around. We ate at La Tannerie. Good Restaurant. Choucroute cooked in Champagne. Served by a waiter in white gloves. Very posh. Took a day trip over the river to Germany. Toured around the Black Forest in a chauffeur driven car. We visited the Casino At Baden Baden. Her family knew someone there. Treated like kings we were. Given a horse drawn carriage for the day.

We went to stay with Tony. He had a bar and a restaurant on the Costa now. He was looking at another hotel. He spoiled us. I had a suntan in winter. We bought endless clothes. We hardly ever ate in. Somehow it didn't seem to be enough for her.

We went to stay with her family. We went hunting. In the mountains. With the chief of police. Shooting rabbits with AK47's. They gave me an old sten gun. Couldn't hit a thing. They thought it was hilarious.

We went fishing . Drinking champagne in the bay. They played Elvis and Tony Bennett on their Boat. It sounded good in the sun.

We bought a house in Hertfordshire. We always ate out. We had wild parties. We had mountains of champagne. Giovanni and Eric came down from London. They got on well with her Theatre crowd. We played Charles Aznavour. We played Les Negresses Vertes. We played The Gipsy Kings. Her family came. Sometimes all of them. It almost seemed like she didn't want me to like them. She had her reasons for being in England i guess. Look after our little girl they said. We went to stay with Tony again. He don't look so good. He spoilt us rotten. He took us to his friend's restaurant. Chose the wine. Blimey. Him a wine buff ? I shouldn't underestimate my friends. Two years earlier whilst I was here, Tony had a little altercation with the locals. Jose and his band of Gypsies. He thought Tony was here to smuggle and sell. He wasn't though. This was a place to hide. That's all. They threatened to cut our throats. Came down and broke all the windows in Tony's bar. We went and burned out one of their caravans. Pushed a car over a cliff. Kinda stopped after that. Until a month before .They had turned up at Tony's place . It was the town Fiesta. They were drunk. Tony had barred them. They shot out his windows. Oh dear.

Turns out my natural father, Arthur ,knows my favourite 60's band 'Love'. How cool is that. We get tickets to see them perform the 'Forever Changes' album at the Royal Festival Hall. What a beautiful gig. Go backstage. Meet my heroes. Signed everything. Wow. I meet loads of people through Arthur. Including Tim Rose. What a guy. Of 'Hey Joe' fame. He does a tour with Arthur. We go to St. Albans with a load from the village.

Excellent gig. He's like a kind old uncle. We have endless phone conversations. Fills me in on the 60's. Saw him at Blackheath Halls. He dedicated a song to us. Oh my Oh my.

So. There I am. Spain. One year later. Sitting there with my girlfriend. In they walk. Jose and Co. This feels like the good the bad and the ugly. Shit. I could die here. I'm on fuckin' holiday. I tell my girlfriend not to move. Take a deep breath. I go up to them at the bar and buy them a drink. He gives me a hard stare. It was one of those moments. Could have gone either way. I tell him we don't want to muscle in on his smuggling. We do not want a war. But we could come to a beneficial trade agreement. They know the Morrocans. They sell locally. A pint and a Gramme at Jose's bar. We know the Europeans. We sell large scale. We don't have to be enemies. He stares at me. Oh fuck. Here we go. I know they are armed. I'm not. I'm on holiday. What a fuckin' idiot. Suddenly he claps me on the back and laughs. OK he says .Tells me I've got grandes cajonas - big balls. Says we should talk. Maybe make some money. Not now though. Lets drink. I'm quiet. This is their town. Finally they leave. I go back and sit down. That was lucky. I don't know about big balls. I was terrified. Not used to that. There were different rules up here. The Federales never came out at night. People were left to sort their own problems out. Like we had. It was a long way from home.

So we set it up.The next night. We take some wine. Drive up into the mountains. Near to Capilleira. Park at the side of the road. Walk into the scrub. There's Jose and his Hombres. They've ridden up on horses. Looks like I finally found the wild west. Spanish shadows. Laurie Lee.
It's the night of the shooting stars. I get the feeling a lot of things are turning full circle. After walking for 10 mins. We reach an old Shepherd's casa.

We sat there. Watching the light show. The stars are brighter here than England. It is lovely. They're all smoking Morroccan dope. I can't stand that stuff anymore. Still like the smell though. We talk all night. Have to. You follow people like this into the middle of nowhere at night. Either you come out friends or you don't come out. As dawn approached Jose and his friends rode off into the sunrise. Shouldn't that be sunset ?. Tony turned to me. Remember this he said. What ?. Remember this won't you, he said. Course I will . He gives me a long stare and puts his arm around me. Great innit? he says. Yep. But I felt a chill run through me. Someone just walked over my grave. He felt that Jose and co. were trying to intimidate him. I said no. I said it's just that it's their country. Their business. They were hard proud men. You can't just walk in here and do what you like. It's not being intimidated. It's about respect. Mutual. We could have a war but no-one would really win. Better if we had an agreement. Who cares if it's in their favour. Ok he said. He pulled a ring out of his pocket. Said he'd bought it for me in Thailand. Platinum with a blue Sapphire from Burma.
Like the sea he says. I think it's a ladies ring but I'm not gonna say. What's Tony doing buying me jewellery ? Strange night. Then home. Grey skies. England.

We go to see Joaquin Cortez at the Royal Albert Hall. Flamenco. That boy sure can dance. Best of our generation they say. Too right. Stunning.

Arthur's on tour with Motorhead and Hawkwind. We go to see them at Wembley. VIP passes. Wow. Get a photo of them all onstage doing Silver Machine. My girlfriend keeps walking on stage whilst they're playing. I think it's funny. The bouncers don't. Get backstage. Photo's of us with Lemmy. It is how you might imagine backstage at a Motorhead and Hawkwind gig should be. Wild. We end up drinking brandy at a hotel near Luton airport at 4 in the morning. Blimey.
Bit of a social whirl you might say. Arthur's playing Guildford Festival. So are Love. The Darkness. Alice Cooper. Billy Bragg. VIP passes. Meet them all. How cool is that.

Phone call from Steve. He's out. He's buying a house on the Costa. See you there son he said. No more England for me he said. Why don't you come out here with your family. The money's yours too you know. It's more like paradise than fuckin England. I tell him i'm divorced now. Fuck i'm sorry son he says.

One of our friends went to jail. In Perpignan. He was caught at the border. Coming up from the Costa with a car full of coke. He had to take a different route across the border. All snowed up. But he wasn't supposed to get caught. Something was wrong down there. Have to talk to Jose and his Hombres. Our friend kept quiet in Jail. He kept alive. Two Germans didn't. Phone call from Tony. Seems that some Germans were tight with the Government in Castellar de la Frontera. Retired Coke barons. Yeah. Like we were retired too. They were making trouble for Jose's operation. That meant trouble for us. But also a chance to be useful. I made a three day visit to the Costa. Two of them ended up in a lake in Andalucia. There is nothing romantic about wrapping someone up in sheets. Getting them into a slippery rowboat. Tying them in big rusty chains . In the dark. Only goat bells and the wind and the waves for company. The government drained the lake a year later. They found them chained together at the bottom. Gone fishing. They blamed local property squabbles. Which there were. Now the locals, and Jose and co. were in our debt.
Our friend was quietly released after 12 months. He kept quiet. He kept alive. I saw Tony's influence. A Costa del criminal didn't. I made a three day visit to the Costa. He was shot in his

pool. Tony told me to keep quiet. Told me to hide this time. Tony said no more Costa. They minded this one.There were some problems. Old London Gangster out of his league in this new Europe. Tony was off to Goa. Senor Incognito. I was staying in England. Hiding my other selves with my other passports.

My girlfriend got cancer. We got her the best treatment we could. Cue endless trips to Hopital Saint Louis. Paris. Finally the cancer was cured. Little scars healing up. Her head wasn't. She went crazy. She got jealous. She got violent. She started going off with other men. Then phoning me afterwards to tell me about it. I never hit her back. Not my style. I loved her. She just got worse. I came home to find her crying. Sitting in a cold bath with a kitchen knife. Cue endless trips to Marseille. It was hurting her. It was killing me. I just wanted it to be right. Which one of us was crazier ? It all ended. As badly as it could. It hurt. I guess i've been storing hurt up for a rainy day. It's here. Stormy Weather. She moved back to France. Her family understood. I was safe. That was the only good thing from it. I Sold the house. I sent her her half. I left everything i'd bought in it. Dishwasher. Freezer. Washing machine. Sofa. Glass top table and chairs. Even the bed. All that oak flooring. I didn't want it anymore. Fuck it. All i took was my clothes. My books and records. The guns.
My head went. Again. I moved back to my parents house in the village. At 39 years old. How sad is that. I'm starting to think i just wasn't cut out to live on the straight and narrow. Events seem to conspire against me.

Punky Suzy died from an overdose in London. She was on the game. My ex wife phoned to tell me. That made seven of my friends dead in three years. From Leighton and M.K. All under 40. Not me. Why not. Oh fuck. Phone call from Arthur. Tim Rose has died. I only spoke to him 3 days ago. He was coming round for a meal. Gone. Missed.

Oh Fuck. Oh no. Steve phoned. Tony's dead he said. Just like that... Apparently.
I had already booked my flight. Tony had said come out to the Costa. There's some 'things' need tying up. Not anymore. I guess i'm not the only one who gets away. He died a very wealthy man at his Villa in Goa .Never made it back to Spain. The Indian government have a habit of cremating foreigners. It saves embarrassing questions. It destroys evidence. It says don't ask for details. Or we might ask you for some. It says leave it. Stay alive.

I made a speech at his memorial service. I cried. I hummed Elvis to myself. I wore the ring he'd bought me. Steve was there. With Francis and Big Bernard the passport man from France. There were people from Leighton. There were people from Luton. They cried. There were people from The Costa who shouldn't have been in England. They didn't cry. They looked old. They watched me. There were people from Holland .There were people from Germany. This wasn't supposed to happen. Twenty years gone. Me and Tony's money in a Luxembourg Bank. I couldn't get it without our joint signatures. They'd probably start asking all sorts of questions As good as gone. Fuck the money. I was tired of it all. Listening to Frank Sinatra. 'In The Wee Small Hours of The Morning'. Trying to drift back in time. Be someone else. Again.

I started going in the village pub a lot. I grew up there. It sort of felt like home. Back to where i started from. Without a pot to piss in. I was in the worst mess of my life. I think it was all my fault. I felt like the walking wounded. Still i've got my old friends there. I make new ones. They don't know the other me. I try not to think about it.

The Landlord's a friend of mine. Adam. He loves Elvis too. Enough said. He was playing Arthur Lee and Love. Great. The White Stripes 'Elephant'. He played it to death. It was a welcome distraction. I bought it . I played it to death. It is very good.
I haven't been listening to much modern stuff for ages. What the fuck happened to me. I always loved music. I guess I got sidetracked. I go horse riding through the woods. Go to watch the Polo matches at the stables down the road. Try and relax a bit. Village boy me.

I had three weeks off work. I went to Australia . It was as far as i could get. I stayed with my brother. He lived in Sydney now. Nice Place on Manly Beach. Sat on his balcony with a Tooey's beer, looking at the sea. We went out to a party. Ended up playing pool with a couple of hookers in Kings cross. Back across the harbour bridge at 4 in the morning. He's got some good friends out there. It was good to see him. I took a trip up to the Blue Mountains. When I got there it was too misty to see the views. Stayed in a Walton's house hotel in Katoomba. Nice but fuck that gets dark up there. Woken by an Australian magpie at 6 am. They sing. Not like English ones. I go out on the verandah and sit in a chair. It comes and sits right next to me. It all seemed kinda surreal. Like I couldn't get my head into gear. Shame.

I was broke. Financially. Fuckin heartbroken. Personally. No more Conde Nast for me. No more anything. Everything i'd had was gone. Again.

I was supposed to go to Spain to run the hotel. I didn't have a plan B. This wasn't supposed to happen. I'm supposed to be rich. Living in the sun with my friends. Oh fuck. Think... What would Tony Say ... No more Costa. Go incognito. For good. So now Tony's with Elvis. I can talk to them both. I am turning into a song. Lonesome Tonight.

Broken Costa Dreams

I got my head straight. I stayed in England. I was alive. I had escaped. Again. Make this the last time. Its over. Maybe I should stop making situations to escape from. For a while i was worried by cars pulling up next to me. Waiting for the bullet from the Costa. They might bother. They might not. I had kept quiet. That might be enough. To be honest i'm too worn out to care. I took my guns to the chicken farmer. He put them in the incinerator. They'd end up in the dead chicken pit. He understood. I went in his barn. I took a last look at the food trailer. He had two now. They didn't have Uncle Yummers painted on them anymore.

I just go to work. See my girls on my days off. Hit the pub at night time. Otherwise i don't seem to sleep too good .I grew my hair. I bleached it. I took the girls to Mallorca for a week. It was the last of my money from the house. At least something good came from it all. Just the three of us. All inclusive. Only three star. Swimming pool. Ice Cream. Food. Swimming pool. Ice Cream. Beach. Swimming pool. Ice Cream. Boat trip. That was the best holiday i ever had. They were so good. It made me happy and sad. I saw what I was really missing.

Phone call from Steve. Come on down he says. Another trip to the Costa. I haven't seen his villa before. Fuck me. It's like a palace. It is he says. Or it was once. Massive wooden gates. As tall as a house. An engraved sign saying 'Dreamsville'. It's a Northern Soul song. Long curving driveway up the hill. Overflowing with flowers and lawns. Automatic sprinklers on. He comes down the drive on his new superbike. It's got flip paint. It changes colour as he gets nearer. That's some noise. I get on the back. He's laughing. Good to see ya son he says. Suntan and gold bracelets. A big diamond in his left ear. Big cloud of ‘Farenheit’. 90’s aftershave. Always the dedicated follower of fashion. Alright son he says. 'Old on . The drive is about a mile long. We're wheelying up it. At 80 miles an hour. Fuckin' ell. What a blast. Over a hilltop and we're there. It sits on top . Views down to the sea. Across the mountains. Wow. This is some place. It's enormous. Parked in front. Steve’s got a brand new Corvette. Next to it there’s a restored Facel Vega HK 500. And a Jensen Interceptor. They gleam and smell of leather and money. It sure is pretty. A pair of Rottweillers stand by the studded front doors. They've got big spiked collars on. Clipped ears and tails. Stumpy and Zoomer he says. Chuckling. They pad over .Bloody hell. They are enormous. Steve has a wrestle with them. Pulls their ears. They growl. They're talking he says. Whatever you say. I don't think i'm going to wrestle with them i say. He laughs. We go in. There's a courtyard with a fountain. Patio inlaid with Quartz. Flowers. What's this, fuckin Versailles? Where's that he says. Good innit . Yep. Sure is . There's Francis from Bordeaux. There's big Bernard and his wife. It's his Facel Vega. He owns night clubs in France and Spain now. And a haulage business. Remember the stag in the YMCA he says. Fuck me yes. Seems like a lifetime ago. It was. 18 years mon vieux. There's Steve's old friend with the scar down his face. There’s Emma’s dad. I thought I recognised the Jensen. I have a memory for cars. Him and Steve. Timeshare kings. Been a while my boy . Yes I say. I'm sorry. Don't worry . We're all friends here. Bygones and all that. She's a big girl. There's a few others that i don't know. We sit down round the big stone table on the terrace.

A meal fit for kings. He's got a cook and servants. Olives. Fish. Steak. The best Spanish Cava. It's better than fuckin Champagne Steve says. He gets into an argument with Big Bernard over this point. But we all drink it anyway. Tastes good to me. Madness are singing 'One Step Beyond' drifting out from somewhere inside the house. Steve does the Chas Smash nutty dance. He's got it perfect. That's impressive. Not as much as his Northern Soul dancing though.

He says don't worry about Tony's money. We'll get it for you. But in the meantime have a present. He lifts the lid off a serving dish. There's a pile of miniature gold bars. Fuckin' ell. Where the fuck did you get that . From the Russians. What Russians i ask. They're all coming down here trying to take over . But we're not 'aving it . Cunts he says. I think Russia is an awful big place i say. Fuck em says Steve. He hands the gold out round the table. It reminds me of something. I can't think what. We spend two days having a damn good time. He's also got a 1968 Mercury Cougar. It's a minter. Specially shipped from 'Ken's Cougars' in America. It's beautiful. It's yours whilst your here he says. What a babe. Let's go out for tea . We all drive down to Puerto Banus in a convoy. I guess we look like what we are. Cruise along the front.

I've got the 'Pulp Fiction' soundtrack blasting out of the tape deck. The saxophone growls. The V8 growls. This is so cool. - Corvette. Cougar. Facel Vega. Jensen. Sunshine. Yeah Baby...

We eat in one of the restaurants. Watching the procession of Ferrari's and Lamborghini's cruise by. Italian shit says Steve. They're so fuckin' naff . On the next table sits Rod Stewart and some friends. Alright son says Steve to him. Alright Steve says Rod. Fuckin' ell I say. This is some life you've got down here. Why don't you come down says Steve. You'd love it. I say I can't leave my girls. Yeah ok says Steve. If you're sure. But when you want it it's here . It's not the same for him. He's probably got more kids than you could shake a stick at. All over the place. Ladies man Steve. The old tart.

Two weeks later. I'm back home. It's cold and gloomy. It sure isn't Marbella. Phone call from the Costa. Steve's dead. No. What ? Steve's dead. Shot in his car . His dogs too. They were hanging from the gates. Oh fuck. Oh no. I sit there looking at the phone. I feel numb. That's it then. The gangs all gone. Alone again or.

Right I say. I'm coming. 2 weeks time. You sort the arrangements your end. I fly down to the Costa. It's nearly Christmas. French passport all the way. Who cares. I get a cab from Malaga airport. I meet Steve's friend with the scar. On the terrace of a restaurant up in Benahavis. I'm wearing a baseball cap. White joggers and socks. Cheap sunglasses. I look like a typical tourist. Course i do. I'm in disguise. I don't do baseball caps.

Steve's friend fills me in on the details. They are not nice. I can't help crying. I know son he says. I know. He's not crying. He's watching me. If I didn't know better I'd think he was hiding something. He's moving to Argentina .Tomorrow. He said it was the Russians. They did him because he wouldn't bargain with them. And he had took their gold. And shot a couple of them. After dining on their boat in the Harbour. Fuckin' ell. Him and his Temper. Bulldog breed. Why did he have to want more. He was rich anyway. His friend says it never was about having the money. It was about taking it. It's what he loved.

There is one in particular he says. Probably the one who did Steve . I know what he wants. Has to be someone they don't know down here. He gives me the address. And the keys to a hire car. He leaves. I open the boot. There's a browning automatic with a silencer. And a rucksack. With sandals, a linen suit and some raybans. The chorus to a Yello song comes to my mind - 'One More Time' - all slowed down. I can't remember the title anymore. Right. This is not about the money for me either. It's more valuable than that. This one's for Friendship. Cunts.

I drive to the address. I check it out whilst drinking a coke. There's a Spanish talk show on the radio. I wouldn't have noticed if it was in Swahili. I am feeling empty. I drive back into town. Park up in the municipal car park. Wait until evening. Walk back up the hill. Rucksack and a map in my hand. Completing my disguise. It takes me the best part of an hour. They should be heading out to eat later. I wait by their gate. I sit there about three hours. I'm good at waiting. It gives me time. That's it. My mind is a blank. Dark. I've switched off my emotions. No room for them here. I hear a car start up. It comes down the drive. It's Steve's Corvette. Those Fuckers. There's two of them in it. So fuckin' what. I walk out from the side of the road just as one gets out to close the gates. I make a show of being apologetic. I proffer the map. He looks at it. I've got a photo of Steve paperclipped to the top. He looks back up at me. Wide eyed. I pull out the Browning and shoot him in the head. He drops to his knees and falls forward on his face. Twitching. His friend starts to try and open the glove box. Hands flailing at it. He's swearing in Russian. I shoot him in the back of the neck. He's sitting there gurgling. I lean over him and hold the photo in front of his eyes. He dies staring at it. There's blood all over the car. Steve wouldn't be pleased. That's what i don't get with people. Why should these fuckers think they're worse than us. Just because of where they were born. Their reputation don't look too good from where i'm standing. Cunts. Like Tony would have said. Watch the quiet ones. Too fuckin' right mate. Too fuckin' late.

I take the keys from the ignition. There's Steve's keyring. It's got 'Uncle Yummer's' on it. Oh fuck. Is this where we were always headed ? I guess my emotions are back. They must be. I'm crying. I'm getting tired of crying. It seems to be part of my life. No more. All over. This is an end. Right. I've got my kids. I'm going home. I can do something different. I'm better than this. I reach down the back of the seat. There's the two miniature gold bars. Still where i'd put them. I shove them in their mouths . Fuck the money. Be a job to sell them anyway. I take off the cheap clothes and the baseball cap and put them and the gun in the rucksack. I put on the linen suit and the sandals and shades .Stroll slowly down the hill into town.

I call Jose. Tell him. It's over. We're all done. I tell him I'll be seeing him sometime. He says I'll always be welcome in his home. I find a cafe. I have an iced Fanta. Sitting on the terrace. Hmmm. I smoke three Fortuna's looking out at the sea. The breeze is not warm anymore. Time to go. Too right. Back to the car. I put the rucksack back in the boot and drive straight to the airport. To a lorry park. One of Big Bernard's man is there. He takes the keys. He gives me a lift to the main Terminal. I get out and walk straight in . No goodbye. Senor hand luggage. I haven't been here. I'm going home.

I'm keeping quiet. I am the one who got away. I have sometimes wished i hadn't. If it wasn't for my kids...I hope they never know what i have thought sometimes. What the fuck do i do now. Try and be a good dad. Maybe i can get that right. The Stooges - 'Search & Destroy', 'The world's forgotten boy'. Keeps going around in my head. I feel like that. But i think it was me who forgot myself. Who the fuck am I ?
I guess there's two of me. Gemini. Like Tony. Time to choose the good one. Leave my bad half down there on the Costa.

Yesterday Once More

I come off a quad bike in my Mum's field. Honest. Broken shoulder. And a collarbone. Cracked ribs. Out cold for an hour. Nasty bruise round my head. Hole through my hip. Me Ozzy and Rik Mayall. Some club. Hospital. Now i'm as bruised and broken as i feel on the inside. Pain killers. I'm in a daze. It helps. I have three months off work. I send them a photo of my injuries. In case they think my heads gone again. It looks much more like I got stabbed and had a good kicking. Warned off. Funny that. Health is indeed more important than money.

I start walking in the woods. I fall and tear the ligaments in my foot. Fuck my luck. I almost laugh. That's a first for a while.

Finally I go back to work. It's like the twilight zone. Nothing here has changed. It gives me a sense of normality. Somewhere to belong. Somewhere i can get things right. Friends that don't keep dying.

I'm 40 now. Into extra time. I'm trying. I'm living in a rented 2 up 2 down.Tucked away in the old part of Leighton. Conservation area. Nice and quiet. Little courtyard garden. I can see the church tower all lit up at night. Makes me think of Bordeaux. Belongs to some friends from the village. It's in a right state. It needs revamping. Like me. They've let me have it cheap. People can be very kind. It gives me something to concentrate on. Paint. Tiles. Worktops. Quick results. Luckily i have an old friend who's a builder. He's great. Bless him.

It's gonna be a proper little palace. Anyway I kinda like living somewhere where you can hear the wind blow and the gutters overflow when it rains. It feels real.

I'm lost in music. I play it all. I have a mountain of CD's and Vinyl. I don't find any answers in there anymore. It's been the soundtrack to my life. Maybe i should stop listening to it all. But i haven't got anything else. What should i do . Sit in silence ? I'm listening to old stuff. Little Richard. The Beatles. Joan Baez. Neil Diamond. Sweet. Slade. T Rex. My records from when i was little. When things were simple. Still borrowing emotions from the songs i guess. Maybe if i listen enough i can start me again. With a clean slate. Maybe if I don't I could be a real person. Instead of me. I think that once people have written songs and put them out on disc, we can make of them whatever we want. That's what I did. Not being old enough to leave home and make my own way, I chose the lyrics that hit home, for one reason or another, and invented someone. I escaped from myself. Does that make me a fake ? Does it matter ? Like Gloria Gaynor sang 'I am what I am'…….

I drank too much. I smoked too much. The Eagles sang - 'Some drink to remember, Some drink to forget' I was just drinking. To a new future. I kept going until it arrived. My Shoulder got better. And my ankle. I started running through the woods . Ten miles sometimes. I kinda wanted to just keep going. For ever. I would've if it wasn't for my kids.

I go to Bordeaux for a weekend. Stay with Francis. We have a lovely time. He spoils me. Why didn't i ever notice what a lovely city that is. Up to St. Emilion for Lunch. Driving through the vineyards. Stopping to pick up cases of wine that Francis ordered last year. Life goes on. Sitting out in his garden eating supper with his friends. Big Bernard. Max the Basque. Wine. Cognac. Cigars. I feel safe. This is like a different world. You know what - i like France. Not tainted like Spain. The Atlantic washes everything clean each night. Not like the Med. Joie de vivre. That's what i want.

Finally i'm starting to feel honest. I'm still here. My children are the best thing I've ever had. They are the best thing anyone ever has. I wish i'd known that. I'm trying to be a good dad. In absentia. I make them laugh a lot. I see them every week. Their mum's Fella is rich. Big extension to the house. Porsche. They're getting married. I miss my ex wife. The way it was. I miss my ex girlfriend. The way it wasn't. I miss Tony. I miss Steve. I seem to have a long list of people i miss. The further back i look the more there are. Was it all somehow my fault? Yes. It was my choice. Once upon a time. But I never realised. I missed out on a normal life. I'm starting to think i should have done it all for the money after all. Sure would be handy now. Yes indeedy.

I get a letter from Jose. Inside is a picture of a big Spanish dagger stuck in a table. He's written 'Pensardo en ti' – Thinking of you. Very funny. I send him a photo of myself with a 12 Bore over my shoulder, write 'Hasta la Huego Amigo' on it. Ho Ho. I'll go see him in the summer.

I've been richer. Owned nicer places to live. Flash cars. You know what ? I'm still a walking cliché - Money never made me happy. I'm trying to forget my past . There were many times when No one thought less of me than I did. I'm trying to invent a better person. I still have enough time to make it right. I want it. I'm even starting to play guitar again. First time since punk days. Fuck me i can hardly play a note anymore. No rock for me. I'm learning Flamenco. Still dreaming of Spain. On my bedside table sits a copy of Laurie Lee's 'When i walked out one summer's morning'. A pair of Tony's old leather boxing gloves. Steve's uncle yummer's keyring. I got his collection of Northern Soul 45's too. Sent home from Spain. And I wear my Sapphire ring. I'm listening to Loretta Lynn's new album, -Van Lear Rose, with Jack White, it's great ,and Iris Dement's new LP – Lifeline. 'God walks the dark hills, to show me the way'. Well, someone sure does. It's hauntingly beautiful. Country Rock and Mountain Gospel ? Blimey. Hey - It was good enough for Elvis. Cesaria Evora and Mariza. Fado music sung in Portugese Creole. Drift away baby. I still listen to all my Tom Waits too. Dark nostalgic poetry. And Donna Summer and her Disco fantasyland. One big party that I missed out on. A mountain of Northern Soul records. Happy music.

Finale

One thing i know. I'm good at surviving. I know when something's over. I finally feel almost happy. It's like leaving home at 16 with nothing again, except of course i'm 40. Divorced with two kids. You've got to laugh really.

I've taken up Salsa dancing. I love it. Makes me think about Steve though. Me and my little girls dance in the front room. I've had to buy Tony Christie's 'Amarillo' for them. We all sing along. I can remember it on Radio 1 the first time around. A lifetime ago. I must be getting old after all. Never expected to. Never had a plan for it.

I've started more horse riding lessons too. With Ivan. 30 years since my last one. He's 60 now. I can ride ok, but there's riding and then there's riding. My girls have lessons .They will soon be better than me. They want to come riding with me in the mountains. Maybe not Spain though. When I was little we used to jump on any horse in the fields. Ride them bareback. Just hang onto their manes and go. Tried it on a cow once. Mistake. Only the once though. Playing cowboys. I remember one time I slid around the horses neck. Hanging on for life, It's hooves thundering in front of me. Scared me that did. That was when my Mum decided to get me lessons with Ivan. I was 9. On my 10th Birthday she got Marilyn from the stables to come to our door with a big white horse. Blond hair. Blue eyes. Blue Jeans. 70's babe. You should see her niece. Took me all around the village. I felt like a king.

I've had a few girlfriends in the last couple of years. Doesn't seem to work out. Not really surprised. Maybe I should just go it alone now. That'll be novel. Probably best.

There's a song on Don Maclean's American Pie LP. Crossroads. The Lyric keeps going round in my head. Sort of all roads lead to Rome thing. Seems apt. I'd like to have said Edith Piaf's 'Non, je ne regrette rien' but that wouldn't be true. I do.

It bears reading. It didn't bear living...There were a lot of good times. I try to remember them. Mostly i try to forget. This adoption thing always left me feeling like a foreigner in my own country. Where I was supposed to fit. Maybe that's why I love Spain and France. I don't mind feeling foreign over there. I feel at home somehow. Anonymous. I've always been an outsider. It wasn't a pose. I was born like it. Reckon I'll die like it too. Not just yet though. I'm not finished.

I go and stay with Mattie and Hann. They live in the country now. Near my friend Adam, who left the village pub. Nice weekend. I see Douggie and Neeta a lot. They live in the country too. Nice place. Pool. Merc. Bikes. Our children play together. I see Pigsy . He lives in the country. He races classic cars. Still see Spon too. UK Decay are having a well deserved revival of sorts. Old friends. People I love. Feel safe with. Feel like I belong. I take my little girls to see Joaquin Cortez at the Albert Hall.I take them backstage to a Love gig. What a lovely bunch of guys. What a gig. The girls think it's great. It is. I am lucky. They are little angels. I finally found 'ma raison d'etre'.

What else ? I speak fluent French and passable Spanish. None of the schools I went to taught me. I have no interest in drugs anymore. Haven't touched them in 16 years. Life is the best teacher. Just a case of being able to hold on and ride the bumps.

You know, ever since I was little Mum and Dad dressed me in designer gear. I have a photo of me playing in the garden aged about 6. I've got a Brian Jones bob and a miniature one of those ruffled front shirts you wear with a dinner suit. For playing in the garden ? Another in green high waister flares. High heeled spoon shoes. Big collared orange shirt. About 1972 I think. Aged eight. Very Glam. Designer baby me. Over the years I have grown to love clothes. Not because I'm trying to say anything. I just like them that's all. Retail therapy ? I don't know. Ask my poor bank manager....Disguise more like. Not sure who's under it any more. Not sure I care.

Anyway. July. I am sitting on a boat. 39 degrees. Ten miles off the coast of Marbella eating breakfast. The sea is smooth as glass and warm like a bath. Managed to waterski earlier. We saw dolphins and pilot whales on the way out. You see even now I'm not without friends. I am lucky. I'm not done with Spain either. I like it here. Cabopino. More small and pretty and less naff than Puerto Banus. Back to the villa and out to Vincent's restaurant later. Life sure could be worse. I am lucky.

So. There you have it. Quite what anyone reading all this will think of me I really don't know. I never did anything bad out of malice. Sometimes I did bad things for good reasons, like love and loyalty. What else is there ? I'd do them again if I had to. When I read this and look back, I think I see 25 years of stupid . But then sometimes I don't think too good. I don't know. Hey, what can I tell you, I was born blond. I was the little boy who's mummy and daddy didn't want him. Gave him away.
I think I was the price of fame. I think I was lucky to get out of it. Grew up with people who wanted me. I would have been the son of the king of the Hippies. The God of Hellfire. Guess that would have made me the Prince of Darkness. I'm trying to give it up though. Hmm... He sang 'I put a spell on you'. I've got that tattooed on my shoulder. In French - 'Ensorcele'. Someone's sure been looking after me. A spell would've done it. Anyway, it doesn't matter anymore. I'm a 42 year old man now. The past finally seems a long way away. There's a future in front of me. Like Mr. Wilde I may be in the gutter, but I'm looking up at the stars.

I have found that love and peace can be elusive things. I'm trying to live the sort of life where I might find them.

Glass half full and I ain't finished yet.

That's it. Yeah baby...

Note ;

This book is Faction. Some places and names and events are real. Some are not. Some are allegorical. No offence meant to anyone who thinks they recognise themselves. Life's too damn short.

My thanks go to ;

Mum and Dad,

Douggie & Neeta, Mr. T, Hann & Matt, Paul the Photographer, Steve Spon, Jose and the Costa Crew, The Village boys,
All those others who made this story, but did not make it this far, you are missed,

Lt. Colonel A.J. Chadwick and Greasy Fletch, the best teachers anyone ever had,

Mr.Cas Billy and Mr.Michael Clarke, the best managers anyone ever had, who stood by me whilst all around me fell,
Checkout www.ukdecay.co.uk for further info.
and last but not least,

Mr. John Wallace and Big Pete Gibson for their help in formatting this book, and 'LuLu.Com' for putting it out there.
J x.

www.ingramcontent.com/pod-product-compliance
Ingram Content Group UK Ltd.
Pitfield, Milton Keynes, MK11 3LW, UK
UKHW012233240726
13966UKWH00003B/1071

9 781847 532046